Social Media for Small Businesses: Get Started, Get Results, Get Ahead

Social Media Marketing, Volume 0

Jill W Fox

Published by Simple Marketing Academy, 2024.

Table of Contents

Copyright & Disclaimers

Copyright

Copyright © 2024 by Fox Social Media

All rights reserved.

- No portion of this book may be reproduced in any form without written permission from the publisher or author, except as permitted by U.S. copyright law.

Disclaimers

The author has made every effort to ensure the accuracy of the information within this book was correct at the time of publication. The author does not assume and hereby disclaims any liability to any party for any loss, damage, or disruption caused by errors or omissions, whether such errors or omissions result from accident, negligence, or any other cause.

AI has been used to assist in generating the content for this Book.

Introduction

Social media is pretty much a requirement for almost all small businesses. It enables businesses to connect with their ideal customers, reach a wider audience, and increase brand awareness. In this book, we will talk about why social media marketing is crucial for small businesses, and we will share information to help you decide which social media platforms might be best for you.

First, let's look at some key social media statistics important to not only small businesses but all-size businesses. The data below is attributable to multiple sources, including DataReportal, Forbes, BusinessEdit, Statista, and Pew Research.

General Usage

- **Global Users:** 4.95 billion, representing 61.4% of the world's population. (DataReportal)
- **Growth:** 215 million new users in the past year which equates to 4.5% annual growth. (DataReportal)
- **Business Usage:** 71% of small-to-mid-sized businesses use social media to market themselves, and of those who do so, 52% post at least daily. (BusinessEdit)
- **Customer Expectations:** 63% of customers actually expect companies to offer customer service through their social media. (BusinessEdit)
- **Average Daily Use:** 151 minutes per day. (Statista)

Platforms

- **Top Platform:** Facebook with 3.03 billion monthly active

users. (DataReportal)
- **Other Leading Platforms:** YouTube (2.49 billion), Instagram (2 billion), TikTok (1.22 billion). (DataReportal)

Business Impact

- **Business Users:** 77% of businesses use social media. (Forbes)
- **Brand Followers:** 90% of users follow at least one brand. (Forbes)
- **Social Commerce:** 76% of users have purchased something they saw on social media. (Forbes)

Additional Insights

- **Mobile Domination:** Over 90% of social media access is through mobile devices. (Statista)
- **Video Content Rising:** Short-form video platforms like TikTok, Instagram Reels, and YouTube Shorts are seeing explosive growth. (Forbes)
- **Gen Z & Millennials:** Lead in social media usage and engagement. (Pew Research)
- **Privacy Concerns:** Users are increasingly cautious about data privacy and security on social media. (Pew Research)

These statistics highlight the importance of a multi-platform approach to social media marketing and the need for businesses to adapt and evolve their strategies to keep up with current social media trends and evolving user behaviors.

Not only because of the numbers, but social media marketing can offer numerous benefits for small business owners. In the balance of this eBook, we show you some of the other reasons you should be utilizing social media for your business as well as going into detail on the top four platforms that we feel most benefit small business marketing.

Part 1. Overview | Chapter 1. Why Use Social Media for Your Small Business?

There are many reasons to use social media for your small business. In this chapter, we discuss some of the main reasons.

Improved Visibility and Brand Awareness

The statistics show us the vast number of people who use social media, with many of them being active every day! By consistently creating and posting good content, small businesses can attract potential customers. Unlike traditional marketing, you can specifically target demographics, interests, and behaviors that best match your ideal customer, ensuring your message reaches the right people.

Cost-Effective Marketing

Compared to traditional options like radio or TV ads, social media marketing is often more cost-effective. By creating a business page on the social media platforms that your ideal customers are most likely to use, you have the opportunity to share helpful content that will enable you to attract potential buyers to your business. Most platforms provide organic reach through useful/helpful content, and paid advertising options can be highly targeted and budget-friendly, maximizing your return on investment. Social media offers a much more affordable way to reach your audience than traditional marketing does.

Engagement and Relationship Building

One of the benefits of social media is that people can interact with your content by liking it, sharing it, or commenting on it. This allows you to begin conversations with your potential customers, answering their questions and helping them to get to know your business better. By properly and consistently using social media, small businesses can attract customers, and build both relationships and brand loyalty. This personalized approach fostering loyalty will encourage repeat business, turning casual followers into passionate brand advocates. It will also lead to valuable feedback, insights, and word-of-mouth referrals.

Targeted Advertising and Analytics

A consistent social media presence puts your brand front and center, keeping you in the minds of potential customers. Engaging content, interacting with users, and building a community, foster brand recognition and trust, making your business a familiar and reliable choice. Social media platforms offer easy methods to target your ideal customers with paid ads. They also offer especially useful analytics to help you see which of your ads is working best, and additional information about the people who are clicking on your ads. Small business owners can track metrics such as reach (the number of people who see your content,) engagement (likes, comments & shares,) and conversions (sales,) helping them refine their strategies for better results.

Competitive Advantage

Many businesses, including competitors, are actively utilizing social media for marketing. Businesses that consistently post useful information, and reply to their messages and comments, can stand out amongst the competition. Doing so can also help your potential clients see you as a leader in your industry. Social media analytics provide valuable data on who is interacting with your content, which posts resonate with them, and how effective your campaigns (ads) are. This data allows you to tailor your message, refine your strategy, and improve your overall business performance.

In summary, leveraging social media for marketing can provide small business owners with cost-effective opportunities to increase visibility, engage with their audience, target specific demographics, and gain a competitive advantage in the market.

"Not advertising on social media is like hosting a party and not sending out invitations – you might have a great time, but nobody else will know about it."

Hopefully by this point in the book you can see the importance of using social media to market your small business.

There are social media platforms that are suited to almost all businesses. Facebook, Instagram, LinkedIn, YouTube, TikTok, Pinterest, and "X" {formally Twitter} are some of the top social media platforms. Each one is different in style, features, and how they display their content.

The more you know about your audience, the better you'll be able to create a strong social media marketing strategy. Think about where your ideal customers are most likely to be online. Are they professionals searching for a job, or information on their field of work (LinkedIn)? Do they engage more with visually appealing content (Instagram, Pinterest)? Are they looking for quick, witty updates ("X")? Knowing your audience, what their pain points are, and what they are looking for, will help you determine which are the best social media platforms for your small business.

Fortunately, you do not have to guess who your audience is; you can use various tools to gather valuable insights. Social media analytics will help you to learn more about your audience. Surveys and polls on social media platforms can help you to learn important facts about your potential customers.

Remember, quality trumps quantity. It is better to be active and engaging on a few platforms than to spread yourself too thin trying to post to all of them. Consistency and authenticity are key to building a loyal online community. Start by using two social media platforms. Since we all have limited hours in the day, it is important to focus your efforts where they can be most effective.

In the next few chapters, we will provide an overview of seven social media platforms that could benefit your business, highlighting a few of the pros and cons. In the later chapters, Part 2 through Part 5, we will go into detail discussing each of the four social media platforms we feel provide the most value for small business marketing; Facebook, Instagram, LinkedIn, and YouTube.

Chapter 2. Facebook

Welcome to the realm of Facebook, a social media behemoth that boasts billions of active users. In this chapter, we will unravel the mysteries of Facebook marketing, guiding you on creating a compelling business page, leveraging Facebook groups, and harnessing the power of advertising.

Creating a Compelling Business Page

Your Facebook business page is the digital storefront of your small business. Make sure you take the time to tailor your page to your business. Add a cover photo, upload your business logo as your profile picture, and complete all the information that pertains to your business. Consistency in branding, including visuals and messaging, helps build a recognizable online identity.

Leveraging Facebook Groups for Community Engagement

Facebook groups provide a unique space for community building. You can either join Facebook groups in your industry or create your own. Answer other peoples' questions, join in discussions, or provide helpful information. This engagement positions you as an authority in your field and establishes a sense of community around your brand.

Advertising Options and Targeting on Facebook

Facebook's advertising capabilities are powerful tools for small businesses. Whether it is boosting posts (turning a post into an ad,) creating targeted ads, or utilizing retargeting strategies (targeting people who have visited your website,) Facebook allows you to reach specific audiences based on demographics, interests, and behaviors. Understanding your audience, as discussed in Chapter 1, becomes crucial for effective ad targeting.

You can test the various ad formats that Facebook offers to see which works best for your business. Make sure you monitor your ads' analytics. Continue to tweak your ads to improve their performance.

Pros:

- **Gigantic User Base:** Facebook is still the largest social media platform in the world and has the most active users.
- **Diverse Advertising Options:** Robust advertising platform with targeted options for businesses.
- **Community Building:** Facilitates the creation of groups and pages to build a community around your brand or your industry.

Cons:

- **Organic Reach Challenges:** Changes in algorithms (mathematical rules that determine what content is shown to users) have led to decreased organic reach (the number of people who see a post, not including paid ads) for business pages.
- **Aging User Demographic:** The platform's user base is aging, with younger audiences favoring other platforms.

Chapter 3. Instagram

Welcome to the visually stunning world of Instagram! In this chapter, we will explore strategies to optimize your Instagram profile for business, master the art of visual storytelling, and uncover the potential of Instagram advertising.

Optimizing Your Instagram Profile for Business

Your Instagram profile is your business card on this visually oriented platform. Create your bio carefully, as there is a character limit. Make sure you talk about what your business does, who you do it for, and what the outcome is of someone using your product or service. Your bio is the only place on your Instagram account where you can have a link. Use the link to send people to the most important location. Consistency in your visual style, colors, and voice enhances brand recognition.

Visual Storytelling and Content Creation Tips

Instagram thrives on compelling visuals. Post images, carousels, and videos that are eye-catching, and represent your small business. Do not forget to show your team, how your product is created, and other interesting behind-the-scenes images and videos. Experiment with Instagram Stories and Reels to keep your content dynamic and in line with current trends.

Instagram Reels

Instagram Reels are short videos that are displayed in either the posts, reels, or stories sections of the Instagram newsfeed. Below are some key points about Instagram Reels:

- **Length:** These short videos can be up to 60 seconds long.
- **Creation:** Users can film or upload video clips, edit them, add sounds or effects, and then share them on the app.
- **Purpose:** Reels are a fun way to show behind-the-scenes footage, introduce your team, teach a quick "how to," or make your viewers laugh. To make them even more entertaining, you can add music, voice-over, text, stickers, and filters, as well.
- **Trending:** Your Reels could be featured on the Explore page of Instagram, where a huge audience can see them.
- **Original Audio:** When you post a reel on a public account, anyone on Instagram can use your original audio, in their video. When the new video is shared, it will show the username of the person who created it.

Instagram Advertising and Influencer Collaborations

Instagram offers various advertising options, from photo and video ads to carousel and collection ads. Decide what is most important; brand awareness, conversations, sales, etc., and choose the corresponding campaign objective. Leverage Instagram's powerful targeting options to reach your ideal audience.

Consider influencer collaborations (working with someone in your industry who has a large audience) to extend your reach. Choose influencers whose audience and values match your brands'. Since most influencers have active followers, that is a great way to get your business in front of more of your ideal customers.

Pros:

- **Visual Appeal:** Instagram is ideal for businesses with interesting, beautiful, fun products or services.

- **Engagement:** High engagement rates, with younger people leading the way.
- **Instagram Stories:** Offers short-lived content through Stories, encouraging real-time engagement.

Cons:

- **Algorithm Changes:** Similar to Facebook, changes in algorithms can impact organic reach.
- **Competitive Visual Space:** The visual nature means competition for attention is intense.

Chapter 4. LinkedIn

LinkedIn is considered the social media network for professionals. If your business sells to other businesses (B2B), LinkedIn is a must for you. In this chapter, we will guide you through creating a professional LinkedIn profile for your business, leveraging LinkedIn groups, and exploring sponsored content and advertising.

Creating a Professional LinkedIn Profile for Your Business

Showcasing your business on this professional platform is very important. Make sure to optimize your business profile. Add your company logo as your profile picture, add a banner that showcases your business or your products, and make sure you complete all the information on your page. Ask your employees to follow your page, share your posts, and link to your page, showing that they work for your company.

Highlight your products or services and share updates regularly. LinkedIn rewards consistency, and a well-maintained profile positions your business as an industry leader.

Leveraging LinkedIn Groups and Publishing Platform

Join or create a LinkedIn group. This allows you to connect with other professionals in your industry, and/or your ideal customers. Share your expertise by contributing to discussions and offering valuable insights. LinkedIn's publishing platform allows you to share long-form content, positioning your business as a thought leader in your field.

Sponsored Content and Advertising on LinkedIn

LinkedIn offers a strong advertising platform. On this platform, you can even target people by job title, field, industry, company size, etc. Make sure that your ad text, and the image or video you use, are going to capture your ideal customer's attention.

LinkedIn analytics will give you insights into the demographics of the people who are clicking on your ads, which ads are working the best, and much more useful information. Use this data to continue to improve your ads.

Pros:

- **Professional Networking:** Ideal for B2B (business to business) marketing and professional networking.
- **Thought Leadership:** Platform for sharing industry insights and establishing thought leadership.
- **Targeted Advertising:** Offers precise targeting options for B2B advertising.

Cons:

- **Limited Informal Interaction:** Less suitable for casual and informal content.
- **Smaller User Base:** Smaller user base compared to more mainstream platforms.

Chapter 5. YouTube

YouTube may be the most powerful social media platform because video gives you the power to connect with others like no other medium can. In this chapter, we will unravel the strategies for creating and optimizing a YouTube channel, delving into the world of video content, and exploring YouTube advertising and analytics.

Creating and Optimizing Your YouTube Channel

Make sure that your channel name, icon, and banner represent your business or industry. Use a fun, friendly, and interesting description. Make sure that you are consistent with your branding across all social media platforms. You want your potential customers to easily recognize you everywhere online.

Create playlists to organize your videos so that people visiting your channel can easily find what they are looking for. Make sure to use the keywords (terms) that your viewers will most likely use to search for the information they are looking for. Use them in your video titles, descriptions, and tags.

Video Content Creation Tips

There are many types of videos; tutorials, reviews, a day in the life, interviews, entertainment, etc. Use the video format that best suits your brand. You do not need expensive equipment to create exceptional videos. The most important things to remember are that good lighting and good sound are crucial to making an impactful video.

Consistency is especially important on YouTube. Your viewers want to know that they can continue to view new content from you.

YouTube Shorts

Shorts are fairly new to YouTube. They are very similar to Instagram Reels and TikTok Videos. Here are a few things you should know about YouTube Shorts:

- **Length:** Shorts are always vertical videos and are a maximum of 60 seconds long.
- **Creation:** Content creators can record short videos of up to 60 seconds and add music/sound overlays in the YouTube app.
- **Music Limitation:** If you use music from the YouTube Catalog, it can only be 15 seconds long.
- **Purpose:** YouTube Shorts make creating quick videos super simple. You can make outstanding videos just using your smartphone.

YouTube Advertising and Analytics:

YouTube has several types of ads available to choose from. You can select, display ads, skippable & non-skippable ads, or sponsor cards. Make sure you know what your goal is before creating your ad. You may want to let more people know about your business, sell something, or just get people to interact with your videos. Make sure to frequently view your analytics to learn more about your audience and which of your videos appeal most to them.

Pros:

- **Video Dominance:** YouTube is the largest video platform in the world.
- **SEO Benefits:** Since Google (the largest search engine in the world) owns YouTube, posting videos can greatly improve your SEO.

- **Monetization:** Opportunities for monetization through ads and partnerships.

Cons:

- **Resource-Intensive:** Creating high-quality video content can be resource-intensive.
- **Competition:** High competition due to the sheer volume of content.

Chapter 6. TikTok

TikTok is the newest social media platform. In this chapter, we will explore how businesses can connect with the younger demographic, create engaging short-form content, and utilize advertising options on this platform.

Understanding the Younger Demographic on TikTok

TikTok is favored by the younger generation for its vibrant and ephemeral (short-lived) nature. You need to understand the types of people who frequent this platform, and their interests, to make videos that will be successful on TikTok. Keep up with trends, memes, and challenges that dominate these platforms to stay relevant and relatable. Older generations are slow at adapting, much like what happened with Facebook.

Creating Engaging Short-Form Content

Very creative and authentic videos do the best on TikTok. Experiment with filters, effects, and music to add flair to your content. Share videos that fit your company's style, values, and industry. Short-form content should be attention-grabbing from the start, so make those initial seconds count.

Encourage user participation by creating challenges or utilizing interactive features on both platforms. Sharing videos made by your customers is a great way to build trust, create community, and add unique content to your feed.

TikTok Story Telling and Trends

TikTok videos cannot be boring. That goes for the title, the images in the video, the mannerisms of the speaker, and the script.

By making creative TikTok videos, it can be easier for your business to connect with younger viewers. TikTok gives you the opportunity to create videos that align with their "trends." Since TikTok gives preference to trending videos, you can get in front of a whole new audience by participating in the trends.

TikTok Advertising Options

Advertising on TikTok gives you the opportunity to get in front of a very large audience. TikTok's "For You" page shows videos to the user based on their interests and the type of videos that they have interacted with in the past.

In keeping with the style of the platform, make sure that your videos are fun, creative, and authentic. Try different ad formats, and as always, remember to check the TikTok analytics to learn more about your audience, and which video ads are performing best.

Pros:

- **Short-Form Creativity:** Ideal for businesses that can convey messages creatively in a short format.
- **Viral Potential:** Content can go viral quickly, increasing reach.
- **Younger Audience:** Appeals to a predominantly younger demographic.

Cons:

- **Privacy Concerns:** Has faced scrutiny over data privacy and security.

- **Algorithm Challenges:** Algorithm changes can mean that fewer people see your videos.
- **Difficult to Build Community:** With TikTok's quick scrolling nature, it is difficult to get users to perform actions like clicking a link to your website or visiting a product page.
- **Government Ban:** The US Government is considering banning TikTok for security reasons.

Chapter 7. Pinterest

Welcome to Pinterest, the platform where creativity knows no bounds. In this chapter, we will delve into the artistic side of marketing and explore how businesses, particularly those in e-commerce, can leverage Pinterest to showcase products, create visually appealing pins (posts), and harness the power of Pinterest advertising.

Utilizing Pinterest for Product Showcasing

Think of Pinterest as an electronic bulletin board, perfect for sharing beautiful images. Create boards that showcase your products in different settings and styles. Make sure to add descriptions to your pins, and to include keywords in those descriptions.

Pinterest is a perfect place to collaborate with influencers, who can share your posts with their audience. You can also share other people's content about your business or industry, to help expand your reach.

Creating Visually Appealing Pins

Pins are the currency of Pinterest. Craft visually striking pins with high-quality images. Mix up the colors, fonts, and styles of your pins to catch people's eye. Vertical pins tend to perform well on the platform, so keep that in mind when designing your visuals.

Make sure to add a call-to-action, telling people to take an action like, clicking a link, commenting on the pin, or watching a video.

Pinterest Advertising and Analytics for E-commerce

Pinterest ads offer a unique opportunity for you to get your products in front of people who are looking for similar products. Make sure to keep track of the performance of your pins and ads. Pinterest Analytics will give you the ability to learn what is working and what is not.

Pros:

- **Visual Discovery:** Perfect for businesses with visually driven content, particularly in e-commerce.
- **Shopping Features:** Integration of shopping features makes it conducive to sales.
- **Evergreen Content:** Pins have a longer lifespan compared to some other platforms.

Cons:

- **Niche Audience:** Appeals more to specific demographics, particularly women.
- **Learning Curve:** Understanding the platform's mechanics may take time for new users.

Chapter 8. "X" {formally Twitter}

"X," the platform of concise thoughts and real-time updates, is a powerful tool for businesses aiming to stay agile and connected. In this chapter, we will uncover the strategies for crafting engaging tweets, using hashtags effectively, and making the most of Twitter for your small business.

Crafting Engaging Tweets and Using Hashtags

The magic of "X" lies in its brevity, so make every character count. Create tweets that are interesting and get across the information you want to share. Pose questions, share industry insights, and showcase your brand's personality. Make sure you add images or videos to your tweets to help them stand out. It is easy for text only tweets to be overlooked.

Hashtags are used to categorize tweets and make it easier for users to find the information they are looking for. In addition to informational hashtags, create a hashtag or two that are specific to your company.

Building an "X" Community Through Interaction

"X" is a dynamic conversation platform. Make sure that you reply to your comments and messages. Directly mention followers to show appreciation or answer their queries. Replying to and having conversations with your followers shows them that you care and helps create brand loyalty.

"X" Advertising and Analytics

"X" offers advertising options to amplify your reach. X offers ways for you to advertise your account or a specific tweet. Make sure to view your Twitter analytics so that you can make small changes and improve your ads.

Pros:

- **Real-Time Updates:** Perfect for sharing timely information and engaging in trending topics.
- **Direct Interaction:** Enables direct interaction with customers and industry influencers.
- **Hashtags:** Effective use of hashtags can broaden the reach of your tweets.

Cons:

- **Character Limit:** Trying to fit your entire message into Twitter's 280-character limit can be challenging.
- **Information Overload:** Due to the fast-paced nature, tweets can get lost in the constant flow.
- **Content Life:** Content life is very short.

Part 2. Facebook | Chapter 9. Introduction

Why Facebook Is Vital for Small Businesses

Social media platforms, such as Facebook, have transformed the way businesses connect with their customers, offering unprecedented opportunities for engagement, brand promotion, and customer service.

Every business should be on social media! It's important to be where your ideal customers are online. By maintaining a strong presence on social media, small businesses can showcase their products or services, meet their ideal customers where they spend time online, and communicate with these ideal customers.

Having billions of users all around the world, social media platforms give businesses the opportunity to get their products and services in front of new audiences. Social media is especially helpful for small businesses that don't have a huge budget to put toward traditional forms of advertising.

Because it is the largest and most widely used social media platform, Facebook gives small businesses a tremendous opportunity to compete with big businesses on the same stage. Facebook ads offer detailed targeting, and the ability to advertise using a very small budget.

Facebook Marketing Statistics

Below are six major statistics that highlight the significance of using Facebook for small business marketing. The sources for these statistics are SproutSocial.com, Statista.com, and SmallBizTrends.com:

Facebook's User Base: Facebook had nearly 3 billion monthly active users by Q3 of 2022. (SproutSocial.com) This massive audience provides a wealth of opportunities for brands and businesses of all sizes. (Statista.com)

1. **Daily Active Users**: Out of the 2.96 billion monthly active users, 2 billion people use the platform daily. That's 67.5% of users who spend at least some amount of time daily on the platform (SproutSocial.com)
2. **Usage Time**: On average, American users spend about 33 minutes on Facebook daily. (SproutSocial.com)
3. **Small Business Usage**: 77.6 percent of small businesses report using social media to promote their businesses and among them, Facebook is far and away the top platform used. Over 200 million small businesses worldwide use Facebook's business tools. (SmallBizTrends.com)
4. **Advertising Revenue**: In 2022, Facebook's total ad revenue amounted to $113 billion. (SproutSocial.com) This figure represented around 60 percent of the social media ad revenue worldwide. (Statista.com)
5. **SMBs Usage in the U.S.**: During a survey of small and medium-sized businesses in the United States as of November 2022, over 80 percent of respondents said they used Facebook regularly. (Statista.com)

In a nutshell, these statistics underscore the immense potential Facebook holds for small businesses. This book will provide an in-depth guide on how, as a small business owner, can effectively use Facebook as a marketing tool.

Chapter 10. Understanding Facebook

As a small business owner delving into the world of entrepreneurship, understanding the basic features of Facebook and recognizing the importance of a dedicated Facebook business page is paramount for carving a niche in the competitive business arena.

Overview of Facebook as a Marketing Tool

Small business owners will be able to select from a variety of features and tools to help them with their marketing. These include Facebook Pages, which allow businesses to create a dedicated space for their brand on the platform, Facebook Ads, which enable businesses to run targeted advertising campaigns, and Facebook Insights, which provide valuable data on page performance and audience demographics.

In addition, Facebook's interactive features, such as likes, comments, and shares, encourage engagement and foster a sense of community among users. This makes it much easier for your customers to communicate with you. One of the biggest benefits of social media is the ability to get your small business in front of audiences you may not reach, any other way. When a person comments on your business's post, that post can show on their friends' newsfeeds, even if they don't follow your business page.

Social media, and especially Facebook, offer so many opportunities for small businesses to expand their marketing and connect with their potential customers online.

Basic Features of Facebook

Before diving into the nitty-gritty of Facebook marketing, it's essential to grasp the fundamental features that make this social media giant tick.

1. **Profile and News Feed:** Your profile is a place to showcase your small business on Facebook. It's where you share your business details and updates and connect with friends and followers. The news feed is a section of Facebook that's tailored to each person and displays posts from people and businesses they follow. Crafting engaging posts ensures your business stays on the radar of your audience.

2. **Friends and Followers:** Friends are your connections on your personal Facebook profile, while followers are individuals who follow your business page.

3. **Groups:** Facebook groups are places where people can gather to talk about a specific interest that they share. Joining or creating groups related to your business niche can foster community engagement and build a loyal customer base.

4. **Pages:** Facebook pages are very similar to profiles, but they are used by businesses, organizations, public figures, etc. Creating a Facebook page for your small business is the gateway to a plethora of marketing opportunities, allowing you to establish a professional online presence.

5. **Events:** Hosting or participating in events through Facebook can amplify your business's visibility. Whether it's a grand opening, product launch, or webinar, events help you connect with your audience on a more personal level.

Understanding these features is the foundation for navigating the Facebook landscape effectively. However, the true power of Facebook for small businesses lies in the creation and optimization of a dedicated business page.

Importance of a Facebook Business Page

Imagine your business page as the digital storefront of your company. Here is why it's so important for your small business to have its own page on Facebook:

1. **Professionalism and Credibility:** A Facebook business page lends an air of professionalism to your brand. Having a Facebook page lends legitimacy to your small business, shows that you are current with the times and that you are willing to meet your customers where they are, online.
2. **Audience Insights:** Facebook offers business page owners access to all kinds of information about their content, their ads, and the types of people who view them.
3. **Targeted Advertising:** With a Facebook business page, you unlock the potential for targeted advertising. Use Facebook's targeting tools to select the types of people you want your ad to be shown to.
4. **Customer Engagement:** The interactive features of a business page, such as comments, likes, and shares, facilitate direct engagement with your audience. Prompt responses and meaningful interactions build trust and loyalty among your customers.
5. **SEO Benefits:** Having a Facebook business page positively influences your online visibility. Having your small business on Facebook will give it more SEO clout. This can help to get your company in front of more of your ideal customers.

Understanding the basic features of Facebook and recognizing the significance of a dedicated business page is the first step toward harnessing the platform's immense marketing potential.

34

Chapter 11. Setting Up a Facebook Business Page

The importance of social media for small businesses is enormous. The first step in this process is to create a Facebook business page for your company. In this chapter, we'll walk you through the process in a straightforward manner, providing tips on selecting an attention-grabbing cover image, creating eye-catching visuals, and optimizing the all-important "About" section.

Step-by-Step Guide to Creating a Business Page

1. **Getting Started:** Login to your personal Facebook account. Place your cursor on the top, right menu, and click on "Create." Next, choose "Business or Brand" to start the page creation process.

2. **Complete the Page Information:** It's important to complete all the information that pertains to your business. This concise introduction will be crucial for visitors to understand what your business is about.

3. **Profile and Cover Photos:** Upload a professional and recognizable profile picture, typically your business logo. Your cover photo should be an image that pertains to your business, your products or services, or the industry you serve. Make sure the image is clear and good quality.

4. **Adding Details:** Fill out the requested information that pertains to your business. Make sure that you add your

contact information so that customers and potential customers can reach you.

5. **Create a Username:** Choose a unique and easy-to-remember username, also known as your Facebook web address. I recommend that you use your business name, all run together, no dashes or hyphens. If your business name is extremely long, or not available, try using an abbreviated form of the name. You can also try adding "official" to the end of your business name, if the name of the business alone, is not available.

6. **Settings and Permissions:** Make sure that your review your page settings. Consider enabling messaging for direct communication with customers and set privacy settings to align with your business goals.

Tips for Choosing a Name and Attractive Visuals

1. **Name Matters:** The best thing you can do is to use your actual business name, not just on Facebook, but on all the social media platforms you use. By doing so, you make it easier for your customers and potential customers to find you. This also helps let them know that they have located the correct business.

2. **Visual Appeal:** Spend time making your images and videos clear, good quality, and interesting. Keeping your brand logo, colors, and style consistent on Facebook, your website, and the other social media platforms you use, will greatly improve your brand recognition.

3. **Showcase Your Products or Services:** Use your visuals to showcase what your business offers. Whether it's a product

display or a snapshot of your services, visuals should instantly communicate the essence of your business.

4. **Engaging Content:** Make sure you post consistently. Share content that can help your potential customers. You can also post things that are funny, entertaining, or interesting. By doing so you will help to create interest in your small business and keep your ideal customers up to date on what's happening.

Importance of the "About" Section and How to Optimize It

1. **Your Business Story:** Use the "About" section of your page to explain what your business does, who it serves, and what the outcome will be of using your product or service. Share your passion with your ideal customers. Tell them what you love about your business and your industry. Also, explain why your business is different than your competitors.

2. **Keywords for Discoverability**: Incorporate relevant keywords in your "About" section to enhance discoverability. Keywords are the terms that your ideal customers would type in to search for your product, service or the industry you serve.

3. **Contact Information:** Reiterate your contact details in the "About" section. This is a great way to make it easier for your ideal customers to reach you.

4. **Link to Your Website and Social Media:** Make sure to add links to all your other social media pages. Maybe someone would rather follow you on one of those platforms.

In conclusion, setting up a Facebook Business Page is a fundamental step in your digital marketing journey. By carefully crafting your page, selecting a recognizable name, creating captivating visuals, and optimizing the "About" section, you'll be well-positioned to establish a compelling online presence that resonates with your target audience.

Chapter 12. Content Creation for Your Facebook Page

So, you've set up your Facebook page with your logo and a killer cover photo. Now comes the real fun: filling it with content that makes your audience say, "Whoa, where's this awesome business been hiding?" Think of your Facebook page as your digital storefront, and your content is like the products lining the shelves. It needs to be interesting, paint a good picture of your business, and entice people to come back.

Content Craving: Diverse Delights for Different Appetites

Imagine you walk into a store filled with just plain text descriptions of products. Sounds dull, right? Facebook offers a lot of content options to keep your audience's attention hooked. Let's explore some favorites:

- **Textual Treats:** Words are powerful, so craft captions that spark curiosity, tell stories, or ask questions. Share updates, introduce your team, or offer quick tips related to your business. Bonus points for witty humor or inspirational quotes!
- **Image Extravaganza:** Pictures are what catch people's eye and encourage them to view more content on your page. Showcase your products, share behind-the-scenes glimpses, or post eye-catching infographics. Remember, high-quality visuals are key!
- **Video Voyages:** The best way to grab viewers' attention is with video! Create short tutorials, product demos, customer testimonials, or even fun blooper reels. People love a peek into

your world, and videos offer a chance to truly connect.

- **Live Stream Livelihood:** Live video is a wonderful way to be able to interact with your customers and potential customers, in real time. Host Q&A sessions, showcase a new product launch, or offer a virtual tour of your business. Meeting live with your viewers is such a great way to build trust and help customers learn more about your business.
- **Story Snapshots:** Facebook Stories disappear after 24 hours, making them perfect for quick updates, sneak peeks, or behind-the-scenes moments. Use polls, quizzes, and interactive features to keep things fresh and fun.

Content Calendar: From Chaos to Captivating Flow

Ever tried cooking without a recipe? Content creation can be similar, leading to a jumble of random posts. That's where a content calendar comes in, your trusty map to Facebook posting glory. Plan your content themes, types, and posting times in advance. Think holidays, upcoming events, or industry trends. This way, you avoid last-minute scrambles and ensure your audience gets a steady stream of engaging content.

Engaging Content: What Makes Social Media Interesting

Here are some tips to remember:

- **Know Your Audience:** Think about their interests, challenges, and what makes them tick. Craft your content so that it speaks to your ideal customers. Make sure it addresses their concerns, speaks to their wants and lets them know that your product or service is just what they're looking for.
- **Be Authentic:** Let your personality shine through! People connect with realness, so share your story, your journey, and your unique perspective.

- **Ask Questions:** Spark conversations and encourage interaction. Polls, quizzes, and open-ended questions make your audience feel heard and involved.
- **Mix it Up:** Don't get stuck in a content rut. Experiment with different formats, lengths, and tones. Surprise your audience and keep them guessing!
- **Be Visual:** Show don't just tell. Images, videos, and graphics help grab viewers' attention and give them a more in-depth look at your products and services.
- **Post Consistently:** Regularity is key to building a loyal following. Sticking to your content calendar ensures your audience knows when to expect your next awesome post.
- **Listen and Respond:** Your audience is like a chatty customer in your store. Engage with their comments, answer questions, and show you care about their feedback.

Continuing to hone your content so it becomes more attractive to your ideal customers should be your goal. By experimenting with different content types, adhering to a well-planned content calendar, and implementing engagement strategies, you can elevate your Facebook presence and build a loyal online community for your business.

Chapter 13. Growing Your Audience

In this chapter, we'll look into crucial aspects of expanding your audience— an essential step toward enhancing your online visibility and, ultimately, boosting your business. We'll explore the importance of audience engagement, effective strategies for increasing followers, and the invaluable use of Facebook groups for business growth.

The Importance of Audience Engagement

Imagine your Facebook page as a bustling storefront on a busy street. The more engaged your audience is, the more likely they are to stop by, browse your offerings, and become loyal customers. Audience engagement is not just a metric; it's a reflection of the relationship you build with your followers. Facebook's algorithm (a set of mathematical rules that Facebooks uses to determine what content to show on user's new feeds) favors content that sparks interactions, making engagement (likes, comments, shares on clicks) a key factor in reaching a broader audience.

To foster engagement, prioritize creating content that resonates with your audience. Share valuable and relevant information, ask thought-provoking questions, and encourage feedback. Respond promptly to comments and messages, showing your audience that their opinions matter. By actively participating in discussions, you not only build a sense of community but also increase the visibility of your posts.

Strategies for Increasing Page Likes and Followers

Building a sizable audience on Facebook requires a strategic approach. Here are some effective strategies to increase page likes and followers:

1. **Consistent Content Sharing:** Regularly share compelling content that aligns with your brand and provides value to your audience. This consistency keeps your page active and encourages users to follow for more updates.

2. **Promotions and Contests:** Encourage likes and follows by running promotions or contests. Make sure to require that participants "like" your Facebook page in order to take part in your contests. This will help to grow your account and get your business in front of additional people.

3. **Cross-Promotion:** Work with influencers (people with a large number of followers who have an audience who would also be interested in your product or service) to help spread the word about your business. Collaborate with other small businesses who have the same audiences, but sell different products or services than you do. This allows you to tap into their audience, exposing your page to potential followers who may also be interested in your business.

4. **Facebook Ads:** Use the targeting function of the ads to choose the specifics (age range, gender, location, interests) to make sure that your ads are showing to people who are your ideal customers.

How to Use Facebook Groups for Business

Facebook groups provide an excellent platform for community building and direct interaction with your target audience. Here's how to leverage Facebook groups for business growth:

1. **Create a Branded Group:** Establish a Facebook group that aligns with your business's values and interests. This space should be more than just a promotional tool; it should foster genuine connections and discussions.

2. **Provide Value:** Share valuable content, industry insights, and

exclusive offers within the group. Make your group welcoming, friendly, and a trusted resource for people to learn about your industry.

3. **Engage Actively:** Actively participate in discussions, respond to questions, and encourage members to share their experiences. Building a sense of community will keep members engaged and more likely to support your business.

4. **Exclusive Offers for Group Members:** Reward your group members with exclusive discounts or early access to products/services. This not only boosts engagement but also incentivizes others to join the group.

The number of followers your business page has is not as important as the quality of those followers (are they your ideal customers) and how much those people interact with your page. By prioritizing engagement, employing effective strategies for increasing likes and followers, and harnessing the potential of Facebook groups, you'll set the stage for sustained business growth in the digital world. Remember, building a thriving online presence is a journey, and each follower is a step closer to achieving your small business goals.

Chapter 14. Using Facebook Ads

Imagine you're at the mall, but instead of shouting deals at everyone, you can whisper sweet nothings about your amazing products or services directly into the ears of people who actually care. Sounds pretty cool, right? That's exactly what Facebook Ads do – they're like your personal megaphone on the online playground, but way less embarrassing (trust me, nobody misses the days of awkward mall serenades).

Facebook Ads Overview: Your Launchpad to Success

Think of Facebook Ads as little spaces you pay for to show up on newsfeeds, stories, and other prime real estate on Facebook and Instagram. These ads can be images, videos, carousels of pictures, or even text-based, and you get to choose who sees them – from your local dog lovers to coffee enthusiasts nationwide. It's basically like throwing a targeted party for your ideal customers, except you don't have to clean up mountains of pizza boxes (score!).

Here's the best part: you don't need a marketing degree or a trust fund to master Facebook Ads. Facebook ads are fairly simple to set up and run. When you begin to create an ad, Facebook will walk you through the step-by-step process. So, let's learn how to create your first ad that'll attract customers like bees to honey (or maybe like coffee lovers to a perfectly brewed latte – you get the picture).

Crafting Your First Facebook Ad: From Blank Canvas to Masterpiece

Ready to dive in? Buckle up, because creating your first ad is surprisingly fun!

Choose your objective: What do you want this ad to accomplish? Do you want more website visits, maybe additional leads, or simply brand awareness? Make sure you choose the option that will best help you to accomplish your current goal.

1. **Define your target audience:** Remember the mall analogy? Think about who you'd invite to your exclusive party. Facebook lets you get laser-focused with targeting options like age, location, interests, and even behaviors like "online shoppers" or "people who recently moved." Word your ad so that your ideal customers know that you are speaking to them.

2. **Craft your ad magic:** This is where you get creative! Make sure that your headline catches the eye of your ideal customer. Use the same words they use to describe what they are looking for. Think funny, informative, or simply intriguing – whatever grabs their attention and makes them click. Use high-quality images and videos that show your product, service, or business in the best way possible.

3. **Set your budget and schedule:** You're in charge! Determine what your total budget will be, how much you want to spend each day, and how long your ad will run. Remember, even a small budget can go a long way with targeted advertising.

4. **Launch and monitor:** Hit that publish button and watch your ad soar! Facebook Ads Manager lets you track how your ad is performing, so you can see what's working and tweak things that aren't. Don't be afraid to experiment and refine your approach – even the coolest superheroes have to test their gadgets before saving the day.

Cracking the Targeting Code: Reaching Your Ideal Customers

Now, let's talk about what makes Facebook Ads so powerful: targeting. Remember those options we mentioned earlier? They're like super-powered filters that help you reach exactly the people who are most likely to love your business. Keep these things in mind when creating your ads:

- **Demographics:** Age, location, gender, education – these are the basics, like knowing your best friend's shoe size so you can surprise them with the perfect sneakers.
- **Interests:** Coffee lover? Dog enthusiast? Bookworm? Facebook knows everyone's secret passions, so target people who share your niche interests.
- **Behaviors:** Online shoppers, event attendees, website visitors – these laser-focused options are like having a map to your ideal customer's treasure chest.
- **Lookalike audiences:** Facebook can create a virtual twin of your existing customers based on their online behavior, so you can reach people who are just like them – talk about finding your business soulmates!

Remember, the key to effective targeting is to get specific without being too restrictive. Think of it like casting a fishing net – you want it big enough to catch some fish, but not so big you scoop up the whole ocean.

Tracking your results is very important and will show you which ad is working best. Facebook Ads Manager gives you tons of data about your ad's performance, so use it to your advantage! A/B testing (running an additional version of the same ad, and only changing one element of it) will help you to quickly see which images, headlines, and text will work the best. Make sure to only change one element of the ad at a time, or else you won't know which of the changes made the ad perform better.

Feeling overwhelmed? Don't worry, Fox Social Media's training arm, Simple Marketing Academy, offers tons of free video and audio tutorials to assist you.

Chapter 15. Measuring Success on Facebook

Facebook analytics provide lots of important data to help you understand your audience, what they want, where they live, and other information about them. It's not enough to just create and post content; understanding how your content performs is crucial to achieving your business goals. This is where Facebook Insights comes into play.

Introduction to Facebook Insights

Facebook Insights is the name of Facebook's analytics tool. It allows you to understand who your audience is, what content they engage with, and how your campaigns are performing. By studying this information, you can make better decisions about how to market to your ideal customers.

Tracking Engagement and Reach

The term engagement means how people interact with your posts and ads, including likes, comments, shares, and clicks. A post or ad with a high engagement rate means that the ad is working to attract people.

Reach, on the other hand, refers to the number of people who see your content. This includes both organic reach (how many people see your posts) and paid reach (how many people see your of ads). By tracking these metrics, you can understand the visibility and impact of your content. When I say that reach means the number of people who "see" your content, I mean the number of peoples' newsfeeds on which Facebook places the content. We don't know how many of these people actually notice your content, as they scroll through their newsfeed. This includes your posts (organic reach) and your ads (paid reach.) By keeping track of these metrics, you will be able to see how well your posts and ads are working.

Using the Data to Adjust Your Facebook Marketing Strategy

Data should drive your Facebook marketing strategy. High engagement means that your audience likes the content. They either find it helpful, interesting, or entertaining. That's a good sign that the topic of your content resonates with your audience, and you should consider creating additional, similar posts. Conversely, if a post has a low reach, you might need to adjust your content strategy or consider boosting it with advertising.

Please remember that the number of followers you have on your business page is not nearly as important as how many engaged followers you have. Use all of the data provided by Facebook to understand your ideal customers and speak to them in a way that resonates with them. By using this method, you can continually improve your Facebook marketing strategy.

Chapter 16. Case Studies

In this chapter, we provide you with examples of how Facebook can help businesses in the real world. Through these case studies, we aim to highlight the strategies employed, lessons learned, and the invaluable insights gained from these examples.

Success Stories of Small Businesses Using Facebook

1. **Local Bakery Delights the Community:** Meet Sarah's Sweets, a quaint bakery nestled in a small town. With a limited budget, Sarah leveraged Facebook to showcase her delectable creations. By consistently posting mouth-watering images, engaging with followers, and running targeted Facebook Ads, Sarah's Sweets saw a significant uptick in online orders and foot traffic to her bakery. The lesson here is the power of visually appealing content and the impact of targeted advertising in reaching a local audience.

2. **Handcrafted Jewelry Goes Global:** Jake's Jewelry, a one-person operation creating handmade jewelry, expanded its reach beyond local craft fairs using Facebook. Through strategic use of Facebook Groups, targeted promotions, and engaging content, Jake's Jewelry experienced a surge in international sales. The key takeaway is the potential for small businesses to reach a wider audience and grow their customer base through social media.

3. **Pawsome Pups:** Max, a rescue dog with a penchant for bowties, wasn't just cute – he was a marketing genius waiting to happen. His owner, Jen, started a Facebook page, "Pawsome Pups," sharing Max's daily adventures, hosting doggy costume

contests, and partnering with local pet shelters. "Pawsome Pups" exploded! Fans adored Max, businesses clamored for sponsorships, and Jen turned her passion for pups into a thriving pet accessories business.

Lessons Learned

1. **Consistency is Key:** Successful businesses on Facebook consistently engage their audience with regular posts, updates, and responses to comments. Building a relationship with your audience requires dedication and a commitment to staying active on the platform.

2. **Enticing Visuals Matter:** Having a strong visual appeal can be what initially attracts people to your business. High-quality photos and videos will make people feel something and help them remember your brand. Small businesses should invest time in creating eye-catching visuals that reflect the essence of their brand.

3. **Targeted Advertising Works:** Facebook's advertising platform allows you to choose who sees your ads. You have lots of targeting options like age, gender, location, and interests. Targeted ads almost always perform better than generic promotions. Knowing your audience, speaking their language, and creating ads that speak to their wants and needs is the key to success using Facebook ads.

4. **Engage Authentically:** Building a genuine connection with your audience goes a long way. Responding to comments, addressing customer concerns, and showcasing the human side of your business fosters trust and loyalty. Authentic engagement is a cornerstone of successful Facebook marketing.

As small business owners, learning from the triumphs of others can be a guiding light on our own journey to Facebook marketing success. Through these case studies, we've witnessed the transformative power of consistent effort, visually appealing content, targeted advertising, and authentic engagement. By incorporating these lessons into your Facebook marketing strategy, you too can navigate the digital landscape with confidence, creating a thriving online presence for your small business.

Chapter 17. Staying Up-to-Date

Staying ahead of the curve is crucial for small business owners looking to harness the power of Facebook to boost their ventures. In this chapter, we'll delve into two key aspects of staying up to date: keeping track of Facebook's updates and new features and adapting your strategy to changes.

Keeping Up with Facebook's Changes and New Features

Facebook is always updating and making changes to its platform. As a savvy small business owner, it's vital to stay in the loop on the latest updates and features that the platform rolls out. You need to make the most of your Facebook page and take advantage of the ever-evolving opportunities provided, to connect with your ideal customers.

1. Follow Facebook's Official Channels: Start by regularly checking Facebook's official blog, announcements, and social media channels. Facebook often shares updates, new features, and best practices for businesses. By staying tuned to these channels, you'll be the first to know about any changes that could impact your marketing strategy.

2. Join Relevant Communities: Connect with fellow business owners and marketers in Facebook groups or communities dedicated to digital marketing. Talking with other small business owners will help you stay on the cutting edge of the changes and will allow you to see how others are using the new features to connect with their ideal customers.

3. Attend Webinars and Training Sessions: Facebook frequently conducts webinars and training sessions to educate businesses on utilizing its platform effectively. Attending the training will help you to quickly understand the changes and the most effective way to use the new updates. It will also save you time in the long run.

4. Experiment with Beta Features: If you're feeling adventurous, consider participating in beta programs for new Facebook features. This hands-on approach allows you to test new functionalities before they're officially rolled out, giving you a head start in incorporating them into your marketing strategy.

Adapting Your Strategy to Changes

Change is the only constant in the digital world, and Facebook is no exception. Once you're aware of the updates, the next step is to adapt your strategy to ensure your small business remains competitive and engaging. Here's how:

1. Regularly Review Your Strategy: Mark your calendar to regularly review your analytics and determine whether you need to tweak your marketing strategy. Are people reacting to your posts? Are your ads working as well as they could be? Regularly reviewing your analytics will help you to see any areas where your Facebook strategy may need to be updated.

2. Embrace New Features Gradually: Don't feel the need to adopt every new feature immediately. Just try to determine how each update will affect your strategy. Gradually incorporate new features into your strategy, ensuring a seamless and effective transition for your audience.

3. Monitor Analytics and Metrics: Keep a close eye on your Facebook Insights and other relevant analytics tools. Changes in engagement, reach, or conversion rates can indicate the need for adjustments in response to Facebook's updates. Use these metrics as a guide to refine your strategy continually.

4. Stay Agile and Open-Minded: Being flexible is the key to success on Facebook. Being willing to change your strategy as needed will help you stay current and get the most out of your Facebook marketing. A willingness to embrace change will position your small business for long-term success on the platform.

By staying informed about Facebook's updates and proactively adapting your strategy, you'll not only keep your small business relevant but also enhance your ability to connect with your target audience in meaningful ways.

Chapter 18. Conclusion

Let's review what we've talked about in this book. We started by understanding the importance of social media in business and the power of Facebook as a marketing tool. We delved into the features of Facebook, the significance of a Facebook business page, and the steps to set one up.

We explored the art of content creation, discussing various types of content and the importance of a content calendar. We learned about audience engagement and strategies to increase page likes and followers. We also discovered how Facebook groups can be leveraged for business growth.

Our journey took us through the world of Facebook Ads, where we learned about ad creation and targeting. We understood the importance of measuring success on Facebook, using Facebook Insights to track engagement and reach, and adjusting our strategy based on data.

We drew inspiration from case studies showing how small businesses can successfully use Facebook for marketing. The importance of staying up to date with Facebook's changes and new features was emphasized, as well as the necessity for small businesses to adapt to these changes.

This book has equipped you with the knowledge and tools to harness the power of Facebook for your small business. But remember, the world of social media is dynamic and ever evolving. It requires constant learning, experimenting, and adapting.

As you embark on this exciting journey of marketing your business on Facebook, remember that success doesn't come overnight. It requires patience, persistence, and passion. But with the foundation you've built through this guide, you're well on your way.

Remember, every big business was once a small business. With the right strategy and a little bit of courage, your small business can achieve big things. So go ahead, take that first step, and watch your business grow.

Part 3. Instagram | Chapter 19. Introduction

Social media in business is important. It has evolved the way we interact with our customers and businesses – but the importance of social media in business is often overlooked.

Social media helps small businesses to meet their customers and potential customers where they are, online. It also helps them to build brand awareness, increase sales, and build a loyal customer base.

A Little Bit About Instagram

Instagram is an amazing place for your small business to visually showcase its products and services. It's a place to tell your brand's story, engage with your audience, and be creative.

Your profile is the place where you show and tell what your business does, who it serves, and what results people can expect by using your products or services. There are 600 million users on Instagram of which 90 billion are active every month! Whether you're looking to style your photos, tell your story, or simply create a positive artistic approach to your business, Instagram is awesome. It can reach 100% of your followers using "Stories"! In this book, we'll discuss the importance of Instagram in business and share tips for getting the most out ofbhe platform.

Instagram, due to its enormous number of followers and its highly visual nature, makes it a wonderful place for small business owners to display their products and services. All you need is to understand how to make the social media landscape work for you and understand from the start what your business goals are. This book will walk you through the process of leveraging Instagram for your small business, teaching you how to cast the net wider and thereby realize your business goals!

Instagram Market Statistics

Whether you currently use Instagram as part of your marketing strategy or are planning to do so in the near future, we hope the following Instagram statistics will help you appreciate just how great a tool the platform is for those looking to use it for small business marketing.

Instagram's User Base: Instagram has over 2 billion active monthly users. (Statista.com)

Business Profiles: There are over 25 million business profiles on Instagram. (Backlinko.com)

User Engagement: 90% of Instagram users follow at least one business account. (99firms.com)

Marketer Adoption: 73% of marketers are actively using Instagram. (Backlinko.com)

Instagram Stories: 62% of users say they are more interested in a brand after seeing it in an Instagram Story. (Socialpilot.co)

Global Reach: US-based online stores lead with 86% Instagram accounts, followed by 81% accounts from the UK and 75% from Germany-based online stores. (Socialpilot.co)

These statistics highlight the incredible potential of Instagram as a marketing platform for small businesses.

Instagram as a Marketing Tool

Instagram is especially well-suited for small businesses, which tend to rely heavily on word-of-mouth marketing and whose products can be easily conveyed in a visually appealing way. The social platform offers many marketing opportunities for small businesses:

With Instagram Stories, businesses can share videos and images that offer customers a behind-the-scenes look at the processes and people behind the product. Most people are looking for a brand they can trust and get to know on a more personal level. Instagram Stories allows your ideal customers to feel like they are right there with you as you build the products or services they are looking for.

Shoppable Posts is a feature that allows businesses to tag products in their photos, allowing customers to purchase those products directly from the app. Of course, the more effortless you make the buying process, the more products your customers will buy. In 2016, Instagram reported that 60% of its users reported finding new products on the app, and with the addition of shoppable posts, there are likely even more.

Like Google, Instagram has an algorithm that determines the order of posts, videos, and stories that users see. This algorithm favors content that receives a high amount of engagement, so if a business posts a photo that gets a lot of likes and comments, it has the potential to reach a larger audience. Interestingly, a lot of high-profile Instagrammers often engage with their fans by responding to their comments; this creates trust between their followers and the brand, especially since many of them still remember the days before social media when answering customer queries was often a separate department's job. It's worth noting that Instagram's engagement rates are 58 times higher per follower than Facebook's. So, how can small businesses capitalize on all these exciting marketing opportunities available through Instagram?

That's exactly what we'll explain in this eBook. Whether you're looking to get your first 100 followers or your first 10,000, you'll learn how to use Instagram to help your business enhance and exceed its goals.

Chapter 20. Which Devices to Use?

It's no secret that Instagram has more functionality on cell phones compared to a PC. Instagram was originally designed for the iOS ecosystem exclusively. It was the iPhone 4, in October 2010. Instagram was only available on Apple's mobile platform, for quite some time. This singular device and operating system focus allowed Instagram to refine its features and user experience for an unwavering audience — and, in the end, achieve ten-figure popularity in a matter of years.

It's quite different now:

- **Android expansion:** Back in April 2012, Instagram arrived on Android, opening a far larger potential user base.
- **Web presence:** A desktop version followed in November 2013, then a mobile web interface in 2014, with very limited functionality for viewing and browsing.
- **Continuing platform support:** As of today, Instagram now works across a very wide group of platforms, including iOS and Android, web browsers, Amazon Fire Tablets, and even on Windows 10 hardware.

While some mobile apps remain the only way to access full functionality on a case-by-case basis, Instagram's platform was born from a device-centric beginning, and it now approaches more than 2 billion active users globally. The app has continued to successfully evolve and expand beyond its initial device focus, and that pivotal operational transformation has been key to its longevity and growth.

The Instagram platform was only designed to be used over the cell phone. Today, at the time of this writing, you can use it on both a PC and a cell phone. Although:

Each way of accessing Instagram comes with its limitations, the most noteworthy of which include:

On a PC/Mac:

- **Limited functionality:** You can't create stories, use Reels or Guides, or access direct messages. It's essentially a browsing tool for liking and commenting.
- **No posting flexibility:** While you can upload photos and videos for posts, the actual process of posting them is more complicated, and you have none of the editing options found in the mobile app, such as filters, stickers, or effects.
- **Clunky interface:** The PC interface can feel less fluid and intuitive, making for less-than-ideal navigation and content creation.
- **No camera access:** If your PC lacks a touchscreen and its webcam, posting pictures and video is difficult. You're able to take media from your PC and post it, instead of taking it from a device like your cell phone.
- **Unofficial app (Mac):** Many horrid unofficial apps exist for Mac that can limit your Instagram experience to browsing.

On a Cell Phone:

- **Smaller screen:** Viewing and editing can be difficult when trying to add small details to your post.
- **Touchscreen limitations:** Hyperlinks, font choices, and all the other aspects of your content and profile will be harder to manage and control than if you had a mouse or keyboard.

- **Data usage:** Well, if you are running it on mobile data, it may get a bit expensive as the over-indulgent design keeps pulling new content from the Internet.
- **Notifications and distractions:** When you also need to be using another app, the hyper-ambitious, multi-tasking design can be a little distracting.
- **Battery drain:** Overworked phones never last that long and the Instagram design will try to keep you constantly browsing the app if the cell phone is still in use.

Overall:

- **PC:** Best for social media surfing, concurrent use with other programs, and for detailed content editing (though with some limits).
- **Cell Phone:** Best for spur-of-the-moment, on-the-go use as well as root access to all of Instagram's most ambitious features, algorithms, and experiences.

In the end, it depends on what you need and what you value. If more browsing than content creation, this is the best way to go. If you don't have a smartphone yet but want Instagram, then a tablet with a built-in webcam would be best. So basically, it's up to what's important to you. I hope this has cleared up the signature limitations found in both! Any further questions, feel free to let me know!

Chapter 21. Getting Started with Instagram

Welcome to the world of Instagram. This powerful platform will take your small business to the next level. This chapter will take you through the basics of setting up a business account, the Instagram interface, and Instagram terminology.

Setting Up a Business Account

Your first order of business is to set up an Instagram business account. To begin, you will need to download the Instagram App. Depending on the type of device you have, you will go to either the Apple App Store or the Google Play Store to do this. Once you have it installed, open the app and tap 'Sign Up'. You can sign up with an email address or a phone number. Next, you will be asked to create a username and password. Your username should be the name of your business (no hyphens, dashes, or periods in between words.) Remember to be consistent and use the same username across social media, if possible.

Now you can change it from a personal account to a business account. To do so, find the hamburger menu (the three lines on top of each other) in the top, right corner of your Instagram profile. Tap 'Account type and tools', and finally, 'Switch to Professional Account'. Choose 'Business' and follow the prompts to fill out your business profile. Make sure to fill in all the sections that pertain to your business. It is super important to include contact information, as well.

Understanding the Instagram Interface

Instagram was designed to be very easy to use. At the bottom of your screen, you'll see a navigation bar with icons that lead to the different sections of the app:

- **Home:** This is where you will see posts from the people and businesses who you follow on Instagram.
- **Search & Explore:** Here you will find new content and new accounts.
- **Post:** Click this button to share photos and videos to your feed.
- **Reels:** This is where you can view short videos.
- **Profile:** Here you can see and edit your own posts and account details.

Instagram Terminology

Knowing Instagram terminology will help you to effectively navigate the platform:

- **Posts:** These are the images or videos that you share on Instagram. All these pictures and videos will stay on your profile until you delete them.
- **Stories:** These are posts that show in a vertical format and cover the entire phone screen. All stories remain visible for just 24 hours, after which time, Instagram removes them.
- **Reels:** These are short, 15 to 30-second videos that you can creatively edit with music and effects. Now that you are familiar with Instagram's business account setup, interface, and terminology, you are ready to explore it as a powerful tool for a small business owner.

Now that you are familiar with Instagram's business account setup, interface, and terminology, you are ready to explore it as a powerful marketing tool.

Chapter 22. Building Your Brand Identity

In the dynamic landscape of social media, small business owners know the value of having a distinct and uniform brand identity on Instagram, that helps prospective customers find them. Your brand is essentially the face of your business, and in this chapter, we'll explore building a formidable brand identity that includes the critical components of consistent branding, writing a compelling Instagram bio, and a feed your customers can't help but pause to admire.

Importance of Consistent Branding

Consistency is the basis of any successful brand. Think of your brand as an individual – how do you want that individual to appear and be remembered by people? Consistent branding is vital for establishing recognition and trust. If done correctly, a consistent brand identity will ensure that your business gets recognized and impresses your audience on Instagram.

Consistency goes way beyond just using the same logos and color palettes – it includes creating a uniform tone, style, and message throughout all your posts. Such uniformity will help your audience to easily identify your business and distinguish it from the inordinate amount of other content found on Instagram.

It's essentially telling your audience what they can expect from your brand. This consistency makes a brand not only memorable but also worthy of their trust. Whether it's the language you use, the colors you choose, or even the sorts of pictures and videos you post, a consistent brand identity will make your small business not just recognizable, but reliable in the eyes of your Instagram audience. However, make sure to be creative and interesting. Do not build a feed that is boring.

Creating a Compelling Bio

Your Instagram bio is your digital storefront – it's the first impression you make on people who stumble across your profile. That said, it should be compelling, memorable, and represent as much of your business as possible. In this small section, you should summarize who your business is, what you do, and why someone should follow you.

Start with a succinct description of your business. Clearly communicate your niche, products, or services. Use language that appeals to your target market. Don't be afraid to have a bit of fun; remember that you're selling more than just a product or service. You're selling an experience, a story, a lifestyle.

Add your contact information and link to your website (or to a specific landing page). Make it easy for interested users to take the next step, get in touch, or explore your offerings. Don't forget that emojis can add a little extra personality and visually break up the text, making your bio more scannable and engaging.

Crafting a Cohesive Feed

Your Instagram feed is your visual portfolio. It's a collection of images that collectively tell the story of your brand. Designing a cohesive feed consists of curation that not only aligns with your brand identity but also creates an aesthetically pleasing, harmonious experience for your followers.

Start by defining a strong visual style. Choose a color palette, use consistent filters, and maintain a consistent theme. Your posts shouldn't be identical, but there should be a visual thread that ties your content together.

Plan your content strategy. Consider how you will mix in promotional posts, behind-the-scenes glimpses, customer testimonials, lifestyle shots, etc. This not only keeps your feed fresh but also allows your audience to connect with different aspects of your brand.

Always keep in mind that your goal is to create a space that is visually inviting, reflects your brand's personality, and resonates with the kind of users you wish to attract. A well-designed feed doesn't just attract new followers; it keeps them interested and coming back for more.

Crafting a strong brand on Instagram takes enormous commitment to consistency in your bio, in your feed, and in your stories. If you can manage to find the threads that tie all of these components together, you're likely to be able to craft a brand that's visually appealing and resonates with your ideal customers.

At the end of the day, Instagram is all about the double-tap (double-tapping on a post is one of the ways that your audience can "like" a post.) Double down on these aspects and you'll be well on your way to grabbing the double-taps, the hearts, and the imagination of your audience. Don't underestimate the long-term value of a strong Instagram presence for fostering trust and propelling your small business to new heights in the digital age.

Chapter 23. The Art of Content Creation

In the dynamic and ever-evolving world of digital marketing, crafting compelling content on Instagram is essential for small business' success. We'll cover various types of content, share tips for creating posts that engage, and explore one of the most powerful strategies of all — user-generated content (UGC).

Types of Content: A Palette of Possibilities

1. **Photos:** Start your Instagram journey by mastering the art of the photo. A picture is worth a thousand words, and quality visuals are the linchpin to crafting a powerful online presence. You want to exhibit your products or services through high-res images that can tell a story, evoke emotions, and most important of all – resonate with your target audience.

1. **Videos:** So, you've conquered the world of photos. The next stop is video content. Let's face it, video speaks a thousand more words and gives your audience a much more immersive way to experience what you have to offer. Leverage short, engaging videos that showcase brand aesthetics, provide behind-the-scenes glimpses, or demonstrate the tangible value of your products or services. No matter what content you're creating — and the world of Instagram, in general — the key to constructing quality content is to always keep it short, sweet, and effective. You have a very concise amount of time to catch and then keep your audience's attention, so you want to ensure that your message is always clear and captivating. And when video is involved, remember that it may be worth

it to invest in the production of a solid video if it's on brand and falls under the umbrella of what you're trying to convey. Remember that authenticity is more important than high production value. Your audience wants to see the real people behind the business.

1. **Stories:** Instagram Stories are a transient yet incredibly fierce feature that allows you to connect with your audience. And as you start out as a small business, curating an audience is vital. Stories are an intimate and lightweight way to do this in a variety of ways. You can use this feature to share time-sensitive content, you can use it for exclusive promos and discounts, or you can give your audience a day-in-the-life peek into what it's like being you and running your small business. The very nature of the story feature encourages followers to keep coming back for your next update or announcement and it's a vibe that you want to harness as a small business.

1. **Reels:** It's crucial for you to figure out how you can share content that's entertaining, informative, and of course, that captivates and visualizes your brand in the easiest, lightest way possible. Music options? Check. Effects. Tons. Allows for classic super smooth transitions in your video. Of course. If this sounds positive, it's because it is. Instagram marketing enthusiasts, personal and commercial video creators, and just general people everywhere are creating Instagram Reels. There are three things you should keep in mind. 1) Don't make it too long, complicated, or difficult to understand. 2) Make your point as soon as you can — and make it true because brevity and authenticity are everything users want! 3) You only have 15 seconds to convey your message.

Tips for Creating Engaging Content Capturing Hearts

and Minds

1. **Know Your Audience:**

Understanding your target demographic is critical. Tailor your content to suit their tastes, interests, and needs. By doing so, your posts will resonate with those who matter most, fostering brand loyalty.

1. **Consistency is Key:**

Establish a consistent posting schedule to keep your audience engaged. Whether you opt to post daily, bi-weekly, or weekly, doing so helps to foster anticipation and keeps your brand at the forefront of your followers' minds.

1. **Be Authentic:**

Honesty is the best policy. Showcase the human side of your business, share your story, and be genuine in your interactions. Your authenticity will bode well with your audience, making them more likely to share and support your content and brand.

1. **Embrace Visual Cohesion:**

Keep your feed cohesive by taking on a consistent visual style. Not only does doing so make your feed look professional, but it also helps to create brand recognition. Opt for a pleasing color pallet and think about the overall visual appeal of your Instagram grid, but don't be boring or repetitive.

Utilizing User-Generated Content: Empowering Your

Community

Involving user-generated content within your strategy helps to construct a community of avid followers who are proud to be a part of your brand's narrative.

1. **Run Contests and Challenges:** Engage your audience by hosting contests or challenges that have them create and share content related to your brand. Not only will this serve to inspire creativity, but it will also provide you with a bank of authentic content to use for your business.

1. **Share Customer Testimonials:** Turn positive customer feedback into compelling content. Share testimonials organically through posts or Stories, illustrating real experiences with your products or services. Not only will this increase your credibility, but it is a great way to foster trust among potential customers.

1. **Feature User Stories:** Celebrate your followers by featuring their stories or experiences with your brand. This is a terrific way to acknowledge their support, while also providing social proof to potential customers. After all, illustrating the positive impact your business is having on people's lives is one of the most effective ways to convert sales.

Mastering the art of content creation on Instagram requires a mix of creativity, strategy, and authenticity. Understanding the different types of content available, implementing tips to increase engagement, and leveraging the power of user-generated content, will enable small business owners to build a strong online presence that resonates with their audience, driving success in the competitive digital landscape.

Chapter 24. Instagram Algorithms and Engagement

In this chapter, we will be delving deeper into the world of Instagram marketing! We're going to be decoding the enigma that is Instagram algorithms, discussing strategies for increasing engagement and looking at the importance of consistent posting in growing your small business in the realms of this vibrant platform.

Understanding Instagram Algorithms

Before exploring strategies, it's vital to comprehend the inner workings of Instagram algorithms. Instagram doesn't show every post on every user's feed. At its core, Instagram algorithms are complex systems that sift through extensive user data to present recent and relevant posts on each user's feed based on many factors.

- **Interest:** Instagram seeks to display content that is most relevant to a user's interests. Users are more likely to see content in their feed that is relevant to what they regularly engage with, meaning content they like, comment on or share.
- **Timeliness:** Recent posts are prioritized above older ones in hopes of keeping users up to date on what's happening.
- **Relationship:** Instagram places a premium on user relationships. Posts from someone a user interacts with the most (comments, likes, direct messages) are given priority in their feed.
- **Frequency:** The more a user opens the app, the more the algorithms will fine-tune its content for them, personalizing

the platform for each individual.

Understanding these factors is critical in creating content that will resonate with an audience. So, let's delve into strategies for increasing engagement and making your content algorithm-friendly.

Strategies to Boost Engagement

- **Create Compelling Content:** Your content is truly at the heart of your Instagram strategy. Think about every post having to be visually appealing as well as helpful, interesting, or entertaining. High-quality images, engaging captions, and a cohesive feed all contribute to what makes a post great.
- **Use Relevant Hashtags:** Hashtags skyrocket your Instagram game. They make your content discoverable and link your posts to other like-themed content for users who might be interested. Do your homework; find hashtags relevant to your space, products, and business, and incorporate them into your post to boost visibility.
- **Encourage Interaction:** Don't be shy about asking your followers to engage with your content to boost your visibility in their feeds. Ask questions, host polls, or run contests to encourage your followers to interact, and the increased participation will force Instagram to make your posts more visible to your active followers.
- **Embrace Instagram Stories and Reels:** Leverage the power of ephemeral (short-lived) content! Instagram Stories and Reels are great for giving your audience a peek into the more authentic and behind-the-scenes aspects of your business. Their interactive features can give a significant boost to your engagement.

Consistent Posting is Key

Consistency is key to a successful Instagram strategy. Here's why:

- **Maintains Visibility:** Regular posting helps keep your brand visible in the minds of your followers. The more your followers see your posts come up in their feeds, the more they associate your business with their interests.
- **Builds Trust:** The more consistent you are, the more trust you'll build. Your audience is more likely to engage with your content and invest in your products or services if they know they can rely on you for regular, relevant, valuable content.
- **Adapts to Algorithm Changes:** The Instagram algorithm favors accounts that consistently produce high-quality content. If you're keeping up with a regular posting schedule, your account falls in line with what the algorithm prefers—active, engaged accounts.

Understanding how Instagram algorithms work, implementing an engagement strategy that works, and keeping up with consistent posting are the three fundamental steps in taking your Instagram marketing game from your daydreams of success to a serious power play. In the next chapter, you'll look at some advanced techniques and strategies to kick your Instagram marketing game into high gear!

Chapter 25. Leveraging Instagram Features for Business Growth

In the fast-growing world of digital marketing, Instagram has become a go-to platform for small business owners looking to build brand presence. In this chapter, we break down key Instagram features that can greatly boost your marketing efforts — Instagram Shopping & Product Tags, Instagram Ads, and Collaborations & Partnerships.

Instagram Shopping and Product Tags

One of the most invaluable features that Instagram offers small business owners is the ability to turn your profile into a virtual storefront. Instagram Shopping and Product Tags turn your profile into an online store, allowing potential buyers to peruse and purchase your products.

First step: make sure you have an Instagram business account set up. Once you've done so, you can also connect it to a Facebook Shop. Once done, you can begin to tag your products in posts as well as stories to enable users to discover and shop for your items. This feature provides a much-improved user experience and allows for a seamless journey for the customer from discovery to purchase.

Combine beautiful, high-quality product imagery with killer, compelling captions. Also, be sure to take advantage of Instagram's shopping analytics to track how your tagged products are performing and to help you refine your strategy for maximum impact.

Instagram Ads

One of the unparalleled benefits of Instagram for small business owners is Instagram Ads. With Instagram Ads, you can greatly broaden your reach and target specific types of people who will likely engage with your content and follow your brand.

There are a wide range of Instagram Ad formats including photo ads, video ads, carousel ads, and story ads, which gives your small business the ability to cater your content to your audience.

Visually Appealing Content that Conveys Your Message: Experiment with various formats – from photographs and GIFs (pictures with movement) to carousels (think slideshow) and video ads – to determine the best way to visually promote your small business. Remember to remain faithful to your brand identity and craft captions that are concise and to the point. Because Instagram Ad captions can be a little longer than regular posts, you can also use that space to fit in a few more details about your product. Finally, include a creative call-to-action ("get more information", "schedule a call", "click here to purchase", etc.) that will get your audience to engage with your campaign.

Don't Forget to Target: Because understanding your audience is key, make sure you use Instagram's powerful targeting options. These options enable you to zero in on consumers based on location and demographics (such as age, gender, interests, and behaviors.)

Remember, also, to keep track of your campaigns' performance in Instagram Insights and optimize your strategy as you go. Are people swiping up (this feature takes users to the link you added to your Instagram Story), clicking through to your profile, or downloading your app? Use that information to tweak the creative, caption, and call-to-action of your ad. Don't be afraid to stop running an ad that isn't performing well. Always keep customer feedback in mind, so that you can gain a true understanding of what works – and what doesn't.

Collaborations & Partnerships

Creating meaningful connections within your industry is a huge component of successfully promoting a small business on Instagram. Collaborations and partnerships are a unique, but powerful means of reaching new audiences while also reinforcing your brand image.

Try teaming up with another small business owner on the platform. You may share an audience even though you don't sell the same products or services. Combining forces can give you both a huge marketing boost and position your products or services in front of a whole new audience. This will double your marketing efforts without doubling your budget or efforts.

When tapping the shoulders of influencers or complimentary brands for a collaboration, stay as true to how you would promote your own brand, as much as possible. This obviously benefits you and the followers you've worked so hard to round up, but it also shows a level of respect for your new partner. In the end, a genuine partnership – not a loosely connected stab in the dark – benefits both featured accounts.

Try a giveaway with a small group, a co-produced Reel, or team up for a post that feels natural and valuable to both your current followers and your partners. This will expand your reach in a really nice way.

Chapter 26. Analytics and Growth Tracking

Tracking Instagram Growth and Analytics

In the fast-moving world of digital marketing, understanding how your efforts on Instagram are performing is essential to sustainably growing your small business.

In this chapter, we'll dig into the critical elements of analytics and growth tracking, that enable you to make smarter moves and future-proof your biz.

Using Instagram Insights

Insights is an Instagram analytics tool. It will tell you things like; the type of people who view and interact with your content (age range, gender, location, what times/days they are most often on Instagram, etc.), which posts your audience likes best, and which posts get the most engagement (comments, likes, shares.) Available to business accounts, this functionality helps you fine-tune your marketing efforts.

Audience Insights: First, look at your audience demographics, (age range, gender, location, what times/days they are most often on Instagram, etc.) Knowing more details about the people who make up your audience will help you to create posts that are more likely to resonate with them.

Content Performance: Insights will show you which of your posts in performing the best. It will tell you whether videos or images are more popular, and which content topics your audience is most interested in.

This information will help you to adjust your marketing strategy to continually improve upon it.

Engagement Metrics: Keep an eye on the number of likes, comments, saves, and shares you get on a post. Knowing which posts are getting the most engagement allows you to create more of what your audience is looking for.

Setting and Measuring KPIs (Key Performance Indicators)

KPIs are pieces of data that you can get, and track over time, that will help you to see how well your Instagram marketing is performing. Setting and measuring against these metrics is essential for tracking your progress and reaching your business objectives.

Follower Growth: Set a goal for how many new followers you'd like to add and keep track of regularly. If you see steady growth, then you know your audience likes your content.

Engagement Rate: Engagement rate is the total number of likes, shares, and comments that a post gets, divided by the total number of followers your account has on Instagram. The higher the engagement rate, the more effective you are at getting your message across to your audience.

Click-Through Rate (CTR): If you want to drive traffic to your website or other external links, start measuring the CTR. This is the number of people who clicked on your link, divided by the number of people who saw your post (the impressions.)

Conversion Rate: Finally, if you're in it to win customers or leads, get started tracking the conversion rate. This tells you the percentage of followers who took your desired action this year, whether that's making a purchase, filling out a form, or otherwise.

Third-Party Tools for Tracking Growth

Many third-party tools also integrate with Instagram to help you track growth and analyze performance.

Google Analytics: Integrate Google Analytics with your Instagram account for a comprehensive look at the traffic headed to your website from Instagram. Use it to monitor user behavior and track conversions. This will allow you to determine the extent to which your Instagram marketing is influencing your website traffic.

Hootsuite: A social media management tool that gives you the ability to see all your social media analytics in one place. It also allows you to schedule, and post right from the app, and is a real timesaver. Use it to streamline your Instagram marketing efforts and collect in-depth analytics.

Iconosquare: With a focus on Instagram analytics, Iconosquare offers detailed insights into your account's performance, your audience demographics, and your content engagement. Make use of its features to refine your content strategy and build better relationships with your followers.

Mastering Instagram analytics and growth tracking is critical to the success of your Instagram marketing efforts. By using Instagram Insights, establishing KPIs, and making the most of third-party tools, you'll be able to make data-backed decisions, optimize your marketing actions, and take your small business to new heights on this visually driven platform. Lean into the insights, set those high-reaching goals, and watch as your small business finds its place in the vibrant and bustling Instagram landscape.

Chapter 27. Case Studies

In this chapter, we'll explore a couple of examples of how you can use Instagram in the real world, to help market your small business.

Small Business Success Stories on Instagram

1. The Artisanal Marvel: Jane's Handmade Delights

Introducing Jane, a skilled baker who saw her cozy bakery gain rapid popularity through the captivating world of Instagram. Jane's Handmade Delights revamped their social media with tempting photos of her treats, intriguing glimpses "behind the oven," and alluring flash deals for those eager to indulge in a time-sensitive treat. Through maintaining a visually appealing narrative and strategically using Instagram Stories, Jane not only built a loyal local fanbase but also attracted sweet-toothed enthusiasts from the wider region. The key takeaway? Skillful visual storytelling, combined with consistency, can turn a local business into an irresistible sensation.

1. The Hometown Boutique Triumph: Trendy Threads Boutique

In a world muddled with fast fashion, Trendy Threads Boutique, a local clothing shop, found Instagram to be the perfect community for their jaw-dropping aesthetic. After recognizing who their ideal buyer persona was, and converting that style into high-res visuals, Trendy Threads developed an ardent community of fashion-forward trendsetters. Their clever use of the shopping-centric part of the Instagram API meant that buyers could seamlessly make purchases right from the platform, another move that bolstered sales. Lesson here? Understand your fans, communicate what makes you special, and use Instagram's powerful tools to streamline commerce.

Lessons Learned

1. **Authenticity is Key:**

What do successful small businesses on Instagram have in common? Authenticity. Followers respond to real stories, behind-the-scenes details and brand faces. Forget perfectly curated images that feel out of touch with your actual business. Embracing what makes your small business unique, whether it's a look at how your product is made or your team behind the scenes, builds trust and a deeper connection with your audience.

1. **Consistency Breeds Success:**

Regular posting schedules and consistent content creation are critical to finding Instagram success. You want followers to keep coming back for more! Develop a content calendar, spend time testing various posting times, and keep a close eye on your engagement metrics to help you refine your strategy. Consistency also applies to the quality and tone your followers will come to expect from your brand.

1. **Engage and Build a Community:**

Instagram isn't just a broadcast platform. It's a place to build a community around your brand! Respond quickly to comments, messages, and mentions. Share customer testimonials and create branded hashtags to encourage user-generated content. When followers feel part of a larger community, they feel invested in your brand and are more likely to stay loyal and spread the word naturally.

In conclusion, small business success on Instagram is as special as the platform itself. More than a tool for use, Instagram is a living, breathing intersection of creativity, authenticity, and community. Follow the advice in this book, post consistently, and study your analytics to determine what your viewers want to see more of. Be patient and remember that growing a business takes time.

Chapter 28. Staying Up-to-Date

In the ever-changing realm of social media, small business owners need to stay ahead of the curve when trying to harness the power of platforms like Instagram. Knowing how to keep your finger on the pulse of Instagram's updates and new features will also be essential as you grow your business.

Keeping Up with Instagram Updates and New Features

Instagram, like any dynamic platform, undergoes regular updates and introduces new features to improve the user experience and increase engagement. For the small business owner, it's not just a matter of being aware of these changes but embracing them to stay ahead of the marketing curve.

1. **Follow Official Instagram Channels:** Start by following Instagram's official channels and accounts dedicated to updates and announcements. Instagram's official blog, @InstagramForBusiness, and the Help Center are full of information. Turn on post notifications for these accounts so you're among the first to know about any updates.

2. **Engage in the Community:** Joining forums and communities built around Instagram marketing will shed additional light on new features and updates. Platforms like Reddit or Facebook groups dedicated to social media marketing will frequently debate the latest updates to Instagram, providing a variety of perspectives and real-world experiences from other entrepreneurs.

3. **Experiment and Learn:** Don't hesitate to mess with new features when they roll out. Instagram will frequently test

features with a segment of its user base before a full rollout. In becoming an early adopter, you'll gain a competitive edge and show flexibility and adaptability that your audience will appreciate.

4. **Stay Informed About Algorithm Changes:** The Instagram algorithm is critical to how content is seen. A comprehensive marketing strategy, therefore, needs to incorporate regular education on algorithm updates. This knowledge will allow for the optimization of posts for increased reach and engagement.

Adapting Your Strategy as Your Business Grows

As your small business gains traction, so should your Instagram marketing strategy. Here's how to adapt effectively:

1. **Define Your Growth Milestones:** Set clear milestones for your business growth. Maybe you want to expand your customer base, launch new products or services, or reach a specific revenue goal. Align your Instagram strategy with these milestones so that your marketing efforts support overall business objectives.

2. **Audience Analysis and Persona Refinement:** Regularly analyze your audience demographics and engagement metrics. As your business evolves, your target audience may shift, and so should your buyer personas. Sales funnel areas to think about updating include relevance and intent—as someone's reason for purchasing may change as they become more familiar with your business and products—as well as your customers' common questions, pain points, objections, and goals, as you will be aiming to align your content with these.

3. **Diversify Content for a Broader Reach:** Business growth

means diversity in your customer base. Adapt your content strategy to cater to a broad audience while maintaining consistent messaging through your brand. Experiment with different content formats including reels, and carousel posts, to keep your content fresh and compelling.

4. **Invest in Paid Advertising Strategically:** As your business flourishes, consider integrating paid advertising into your Instagram strategy. Instagram has a variety of advertising options such as sponsored posts, stories ads, and carousel ads. Invest strategically to expand your reach and connect with potential customers who may not have found your business organically.

5. **Monitor and Analyze Performance:** It's more important than ever to gauge the performance of your Instagram marketing efforts. Utilize Instagram Insights and other analytics tools to measure the efficacy of your content, track engagement, and identify areas for improvement. Then, iterate and adapt your strategy in response to those insights—doing so is the key to maximizing your return on investment.

Mastering Instagram for small business success is a challenge that requires a commitment to staying informed about platform updates and adjusting your strategy to reflect changes to the platform as your business grows and evolves. Embrace change, be proactive, and view each update as an opportunity for your brand to shine on this popular social media platform. After all, staying up to date can help move your business forward in the digital age.

Chapter 29. Conclusion

Congratulations! You made it to the end of our savvy small business owner's guide to Instagram marketing. Take a moment to reflect on the pages of tips, strategies, and tactics you've just read. Then let's get down to business and talk about the absolute most important takeaways for navigating the social media marketing world.

Recap of Key Points

1. **Optimize Your Profile:** Your profile is your Instagram storefront. It should be visually appealing, reflect your brand image, and contain important information like business name, bio, and contact details.
2. **Content is King:** Create high-quality, visually stunning content that will resonate with your target audience. It's important to use a wide mix of photos, videos, and Stories to keep your feed diverse and interesting.
3. **Consistency is Key:** Your Instagram account should be kept up to date with fresh, new content. This will help with brand awareness and keep your audience engaged. Be sure to create a posting schedule that serves your business goals.
4. **Hashtags and Captions:** Your captions and hashtags are important. Use hashtags to broaden your reach, increase discoverability, and create thoughtful captions that tell the story of your brand, connect with your followers, and generate engagement.
5. **Engage with Your Audience:** Always engage further with comments, messages, and community members. Creating a sense of community among your followers will help them be

more loyal to your brand and help you build a stronger online presence.

6. **Utilize Instagram Features:** Your brand should always be one step ahead of the game by embracing features like Instagram Shopping, and Reels, and constantly creating and testing new types of content.

7. **Analytics and Insights:** An Instagram Insights checkup every now and then will help you understand your audience better and track how your posts are performing. This will also help you make vital changes to your strategy as needed.

Advice for the Road

As you start your journey with Instagram marketing, keep in mind that creating a strong online presence is a marathon, not a sprint, but here's some wisdom to keep you grounded as you wind your way through the Instagram marketing terrain.

1. **Embrace the uncertainty and growth:** The social media algorithm and trends are in constant flux. Be informed and remain nimble. Embrace the journey and see daily challenges as daily opportunities to grow.

2. **Celebrate the small wins:** Whether it's gaining a new follower, getting positive feedback or hitting a new follower milestone. You're gaining ground, and every step forward adds one more brick to the house of your business's success.

3. **Build a real community:** View your Instagram as a community and foster that atmosphere. Connect, be present, and listen to your followers. Your community is your best asset for growing your following.

4. **Educate yourself:** You need to stay on top of the constant changes in social media which include new features and updates, different trends, and completely new social

platforms. Stay curious, keep learning, and adjust your approach to Instagram marketing, accordingly.

5. **Be patient, and keep going:** Keep in mind that you've arrived here in search of information to grow your small business. Overnight success takes a long while. Hang in, and keep keeping in — a little effort, every single day, pays off.

At the end of the day, Instagram can be a powerful tool for giving legs to your business and armed with everything you've learned in this guide, now you can slide along the ever-evolving waves of social media marketing. Here's to the growth, success, and prosperity of your small business on Instagram!

Part 4. LinkedIn | Chapter 30. Introduction

The professional networking platform LinkedIn launched in 2003 with a purpose — a simple purpose, but a powerful one — to connect the world's professionals and make them more productive and successful. The idea came from the professional circles of Reid Hoffman, Allen Blue, Konstantin Guericke, Eric Ly, and Jean-Luc Vaillant, who believed that "we are stronger and better when we are connected."

Member registration for LinkedIn is based entirely on people you know and trust in a professional context, and, of course, the people they know and trust. It's a space where professionals from all walks, and all corners of professional and work life can; connect, consult, share new ideas, and search for career opportunities. Since those early days, LinkedIn has grown... a lot, so much so that the platform now counts over 774 million members from more than 200 countries and territories worldwide.

A Review of LinkedIn's Significance to Small Businesses

In the digital age, where connections reign supreme, LinkedIn is the networking platform designed to propel your small business to the next level. Think of it as the bustling town square where opportunity is endless and where relationships are forged. With more than 700 million professionals actively engaging on the platform, it's no longer simply an archived resume; with LinkedIn, you're an active participant in a thriving ecosystem of potential clients, collaborators, and mentors.

And for small businesses, that means everything; the business-to-business (B2B) audience is there, as are the people connecting them. It's a powerful tool — small businesses can showcase their products and services, connect with potential clients, and build a network of people who can actually help build their business. They can establish their brand, share, and engage. Small businesses can also recruit, and they can learn from just about everyone they've ever wanted to "meet" in business.

In short? LinkedIn isn't just a professional network for small businesses — it's a network that can make small businesses radically more effective; a platform small businesses can use to connect with colleagues and clients, to share updates, and grow their business. And as we continue through this book, we hope to show you just how they can do that.

LinkedIn Marketing Statistics

Below are six important statistics on using LinkedIn for small business marketing, with the sources being sproutsocial.com and hootsuite.com:

- 96% of B2B marketers use LinkedIn for organic social marketing. In fact, LinkedIn is rated the top network for B2B content marketers, followed by Facebook and Twitter. (hootsuite.com)
- 82% of B2B marketers see success on LinkedIn. A staggering 93% of B2B marketers stated that they used LinkedIn for organic social marketing in the 12 months leading up to October 2021. (sproutsocial.com)
- More than half of members' households make over $75,000. (sproutsocial.com) This signifies that the average income of LinkedIn users is high, which could be important for

businesses looking to reach a specific income bracket.

- More than half of members have at least a bachelor's degree. (sproutsocial.com) This means the user base is highly educated, so the type of content that resonates on the platform should be considered.
- LinkedIn is available in 26 languages. This means many global users can access the platform in their native language, so it can be a valuable platform for businesses looking to reach an international audience. (hootsuite.com)
- Revenue increased 21% year-over-year (in constant currency) in Q1 of 2023. This shows that LinkedIn is still growing and is still a viable platform for marketing efforts. (hootsuite.com)

These statistics show the potential of LinkedIn as a marketing tool for small businesses. It is clear that the platform is a popular one among B2B marketers and it has a user base with diverse income and education levels.

Setting the Tone for a Serious Yet Friendly Guide

LinkedIn is for serious business. As we venture further into LinkedIn, we must strike that balance between taking a serious approach to business and doing so with a friendly tone that resonates with your audience. We've designed this book with the understanding that — as a small business entrepreneur — you're looking to make your mark, and yet you may be navigating the complexities of a professional network for the first time.

Fear not; we're going to delve into serious strategies that get real results. But we're here to make your learning an enjoyable experience. Think of LinkedIn as less of a confusing maze to navigate, and more of a puzzle just waiting to be solved. We're going to help guide you through every piece.

By the end of our journey, you'll have learned practical tips, seen real-world examples, and followed step-by-step instructions to know how these principles will not only be understood but applied to your unique business. We've got every base covered; from optimizing your profile to crafting content that'll make your audience salivate, from connecting you with the captains of industry, to you establishing a profile so richly optimized that they're coming to you. On LinkedIn, your small business can enjoy its finest hour.

Chapter 31. Understanding LinkedIn

Welcome to the emporium of digital where business connections are made, opportunities are untethered, and success stories are written. If you're a small business owner with grand dreams, you've no doubt heard about LinkedIn — the professional networking powerhouse that changed the way people and businesses connect. In this guide, we're going to delve into the world of leveraging LinkedIn to market your small business effectively, so grab a cup of coffee, sit back, and let's go on a journey through the secrets of LinkedIn success.

Brief History and Purpose of LinkedIn

Before we get into the nitty-gritty of LinkedIn marketing, let's break down how it all came to be. LinkedIn was founded in 2002 as a platform where professionals could connect, share insights, and build their careers. Over the years, it has evolved to a powerhouse that's now home to over 774 million individuals, changing the way companies interact with their target audience. LinkedIn isn't just a digital resume or a virtual Rolodex. It's a living, breathing platform for professionals that's built around bringing people together, exchanging knowledge, and growing corporations. It's the intersection of the job seeker, the seasoned expert, and now the small business owner where relationships are formed, and collaborations prosper.

Demographics of LinkedIn Users

If you want to make your small business soar on LinkedIn, you need to know who you'll be talking to. LinkedIn does not have the same diversity of users as other social media platforms — its audience is mostly professionals, educators, and individuals just setting off into their careers. More than 50% of users have a bachelor's degree or higher so the bulk of your readers will be both educated and career-fixated.

Furthermore, LinkedIn's largest demographic by age consists of individuals between 25 and 34 years old, followed closely by those aged 35 to 54. As a small business owner, this means that you can connect with professionals who are at various stages of their careers.

LinkedIn's global reach is incredibly compelling. More than 200 countries and territories have LinkedIn members. This means that your small business can connect with professionals from around the globe. Whether you're looking for a local partnership, expanding your business abroad, or simply looking for the latest in global industry news, LinkedIn can help connect you with a world of possibilities.

The chapter ahead will cover the specifics of creating a standout LinkedIn profile, building a strong and diverse network, and incorporating LinkedIn marketing efforts into your small business strategies. But as we take the next step, the question you should keep in the back of your mind is this: What's next for your small business? How can you use LinkedIn to forge the connections you need to propel your business to success? Remember: It all starts with one.

Chapter 32. Setting Up a LinkedIn Profile

It may be just a platform for you to connect with colleagues, other industry professionals, and perhaps a potential employee, but your profile is still a significant piece of the puzzle. As a small business owner, you should always be thinking about new ways in which to put it to work for you, so we have a simple tutorial to create an effective LinkedIn profile for you.

Step-by-step Guide to Creating a LinkedIn Profile

1. **Join now:** Visit linkedin.com and click on the 'Join now' button. Enter your email address and create a password.
2. **Personal Information:** Add your name, city, and preferred industry. This can help LinkedIn to suggest people in your area that you might know or industries that you might be interested in connecting with, but also have relevance to your professional standing.
3. **Profile Photo:** No profile photo is a red flag, but even worse is one that isn't professional. Save the selfies for Facebook. For LinkedIn, upload an image of yourself looking your professional best to be how you're seen first.
4. **Background Photo:** This is the large photo on the top of your profile. It may also be referred to as your "Cover" photo. This should be something that represents you. Keep it very professional.
5. **Headline:** This is your compelling headline. This is a brief professional description that appears under your name. It should encapsulate who you are as a professional.

6. **About:** Your summary is very important. This is one of the first things that viewers of your profile will begin to read and as such is your chance to tell your professional story. Do so and let your personality shine through. Remember to add a little bit about what is important to you outside of work, to the bottom.

7. **Experience:** Add your current position, and then work your way back through time to add previous work experience. Be sure to include several bullet points under each position with a description of your responsibilities as well as key achievements.

8. **Education:** Your educational background goes here. Your high school probably doesn't matter, but if you graduated from a well-known one, or are trying to connect to someone who went there, it may be a good idea to add as well.

9. **Skills:** Add skills that apply to you here. Often, your colleagues can "endorse" you for those particular skills, which will give you more credibility.

10. **Additional Profile Sections:** There are places on LinkedIn to add things like any licenses you have, publications you've written, special projects you've worked on, and much more. One of the most important areas you can complete is the Volunteering section. It's important to show that you have a heart for people, animals, the environment, etc.

Tips for Creating an Effective Profile

- **Make Yourself Discoverable with Keywords:** Use relevant keywords in your headline, summary, and experience to help you get "found" when someone searches LinkedIn for your particular skill set or experience.

- **Be Detailed:** Make sure you take the time to complete all the information that pertains to you. It's important to paint

a complete picture of who you are. A complete profile is also more likely to come up in a search.
- **Stay Professional:** LinkedIn is a professional network, so all your content and interactions should stay professional as well.

Importance of a Professional Profile Photo and Headline

No profile photo, or one that doesn't appear to be professional, will mean fewer views - there's no getting around that. A good headline paired with a professional photo can lead to a great first impression, and in the world of small business ownership, it's easy to lose people if they're not captivated at first glance.

Taking the time to get your profile right is worth it. Your LinkedIn profile is your professional identity on the web, and investing some time into making sure that it is well-optimized and complete, is really important!

Chapter 33. Creating a Powerful LinkedIn Company Page

Your LinkedIn Company Page is a virtual storefront for your business, allowing a unique opportunity to highlight your brand, engage with followers, and attract potential employees. This chapter will guide you through the steps of creating the perfect LinkedIn Company Page, using the best practices for optimization, and highlighting the importance of regular updating.

Step-by-Step Guide to Creating a LinkedIn Company Page

Get Started: Begin by logging into your personal LinkedIn account. Click the "For Business" tab in the top navigation, then click "Create a Company Page."

Choose Page Type: Here you can choose the type of page that fits your business. If you have a small business, you will want to click on, "Company."

Add Company Details: Your company description should be concise and to the point in describing who you serve, what your product or service is, and what the outcome of using it will be. You should also list your company's industry and its website URL.

Logo and Background Photo (also called a Banner or Cover Photo): Your Logo should be the same across all social media platforms. Just like the background photo on your personal profile, your background photo should reflect your business's identity or the industry you are in.

Company Specialties: This is the space where you can list your company specialties. Make sure to use words commonly used in your industry so your business can be easily found.

Location and Size: If your business has a physical location, add it here, along with how many employees work there. This will help your page appear in searches and also help to verify your business.

Create Showcase Pages: If your business has several product lines or subsets of services, you can create individual showcase pages that allow you to promote each more directly to its respective audience.

Tips for Optimizing the Company Page

1. **Engaging Content:** As with your profile, your Company Page comes alive when populated with an array of rich, multimedia content. An effective tactic is to share your company's articles, blog posts, and events. Make sure to share your company posts to your profile, as well.
2. **Maintain Consistent Branding:** Ensure brand consistency across all your online platforms. Your Company Page should clearly reflect your organization's visual elements, tone, and messaging.
3. **Employee Engagement:** Encourage your team members to link their profiles with the Company Page. Employee engagement often extends the reach of your page and makes your brand more personable. Also, ask your employees to share your company page posts.
4. **Use Keywords Strategically:** Incorporate industry-relevant keywords into your company description and updates to boost your page's visibility in search results.
5. **Leverage Multimedia:** Make your page visually appealing by integrating images, videos, and other multimedia elements.

This type of content tends to attract users more effectively.

Why Is Regular Updating of the Company Page Important?

A Company Page that never changes will cause you to miss numerous engagement opportunities. Regular updating is important to make your brand stay top-of-mind among your followers and position your business as a thought leader. Here's why it's important to stay updated:

1. **Visibility and Reach:** Updating with great content is essential. The more consistently you link to new updates, the more visibility will be generated within the LinkedIn algorithm. This will increase your chances of appearing within your followers' feed and search results.

2. **Demonstrate Expertise:** Showcasing your industry insights, thoughts, tips, and successes in a regular feed shows you know what you're talking about. This makes your business much more approachable and shows you as a thought leader within your field.

3. **Engagement and Networking:** Engagement within LinkedIn is essential for many reasons. By liking and sharing good content with their networks, you can ask your team members to share and like posts. By commenting or replying to comments, you can gather useful insights or just to say "hi" to the rest of your community.

4. **Showcase Company Culture:** Behind-the-scenes looks into your company culture, team wins, and corporate milestones are a great way to show how your company runs behind the scenes. This makes your brand more human and allows your company to build stronger links with your followers.

Creating a LinkedIn Company Page for your small business is an absolute necessity to reach your audience. Simply use this step-by-step guide, optimize the page, and update your page regularly to become a leader on LinkedIn.

Chapter 34. Building Connections

How to Find and Connect with Relevant Professionals

The first step to success in making connections is creating a profile and optimizing it. Start by creating a clear and succinct summary of your business, your skills, and your objectives. Use relevant keywords so that you and your profile are easily discovered. Once your profile is ready, use LinkedIn's in-depth search and filtering options to find professionals in your industry or related fields. In addition to those you find through searching, you can identify valuable connections through discussions and groups in which you actively participate. When you do reach out, create a personalized LinkedIn connection request in which you explain why you are trying to connect and what you think could come of the two of you networking. Keep in mind that this part of it is about quality over quantity; your business won't grow simply due to the number of connections you have.

The Etiquette of Sending Connection Requests

In essence, reaching out to professionals on LinkedIn is the same as meeting them for the first time during a networking event. But you get to give off a first impression before they accept you. Most everyone is more likely to connect if they know who you are and what you're about. So, when making a connection request on LinkedIn, ensure that your profile is complete, the picture is professional, and that you craft a friendly connection message. A brief, personalized note can increase your chance of your request being accepted. The general request will not only be ignored by most but it likely will never be seen. Look up anything at all in their profile that you have in common, whether you know them or not – shared interests, businesses in the same field, or mutual friends – just to show that you are somebody who they're more likely to want in their network.

In addition, be patient and courteous. Understand that recipients may take time to review and accept your connection request. If they do accept, consider sending a thank-you message expressing your gratitude for connecting. Remember that networking is all about building rapport, and approaching professionals with respect will ensure that your interactions are meaningful.

Leverage Established Connections

Your existing LinkedIn connections are more than just numbers on your profile; they are potential gateways to new opportunities. Engage with your connections by liking, commenting, and sharing their content. Doing so not only strengthens your current relationships but also increases your visibility in their network.

Consider requesting your connections introduce you to professionals they know and who could be helpful to your business. Don't be afraid to share your goals with them and ask for their advice. Many users on LinkedIn are more than willing to help each other thrive.

Moreover, join LinkedIn groups and discussions where your connections are active. This enables you to extend your reach while connecting with a lot more professionals than the ones in your immediate network.

Building your LinkedIn connections requires you to identify relevant professionals, adhere to connection request etiquette, and take advantage of the contacts you already have. Go at the task with authenticity, patience, and true interest in fostering meaningful relationships. As you navigate your way through LinkedIn connections, you'll quickly see that the rewards extend beyond a mere number on your profile and will significantly contribute to the growth and success of your small business.

123

Chapter 35. LinkedIn Groups

LinkedIn is a comprehensive social networking platform that offers a myriad of unique features. LinkedIn Groups provide advantages that a small business owner like you can use to increase engagement on the social media platform or to boost business outreach. This chapter exposes why LinkedIn Groups are so important for small businesses, how to find and join relevant groups, and some tips for truly participating.

Why LinkedIn Groups Are Important

Think of LinkedIn Groups like this: Instead of a happy hour where you mingle with a bunch of people, the groups serve as a virtual meeting spot of like-minded professionals who join to share ideas, ask questions, provide solutions, and help each other in their industry or niche. The pool of advantages for a small business owner to dip their toe into is deep. For starters, it can position you and your small business as an industry expert when you participate in discussions and provide valuable input. Over time, this practice makes potential clients trust you, and when they're looking to buy their next widget, those clients feel like you're a reliable resource worth betting on.

But it's definitely not a one-way street. Joining in on LinkedIn Groups conversations is a great way to stay in touch with industry news and trends, and thus an indispensable practice as a small business owner. Oftentimes, a 'nothing to lose' kind of mindset can be just the ticket to getting valuable nuggets of information from other businesses in your industry. And collaboration isn't out of the question at all. It's one of the biggest advantages of being in a LinkedIn Group. When you get to know other professionals and take the time to participate regularly, the big old door that's marked 'opportunities' opens. It might mean potential partnerships, client referrals or simply hearing about job openings in a different company. After all, every other group of like-minded professionals has so much to gain from your participation, and the topper is that it feels very different from a typical business 'networking' event. In fact, it feels a whole lot easier.

How to Find and Join Relevant Groups

The first thing you need to do to get the most out of LinkedIn Groups as a small business owner is to be very strategic about what groups you join. First, perform a search for groups that might be related to your industry or niche by using some of the keyword terms that define your business. Next, take a look at the groups closely by checking out their profiles to see where they're located and most importantly the group stats on size and activity.

Also, make sure to take advantage of LinkedIn's "Groups You May Like" feature. It suggests the groups that you might be interested in being a member of based on your profile, connections, and other groups that you're already a member of. Take a few minutes to click through this feature — you'll likely be surprised at some of the groups that it turns up among the most relevant to your industry!

Evaluate their discussions, their rules, and their membership demographics. Choose the groups that align with your business vision and goals, and where you believe you can make a meaningful contribution. When you've identified these groups, send a thoughtful request to join. Once you're in, introduce your business and yourself to begin forging connections.

Tips to Actively Participate in Groups

Joining a LinkedIn Group isn't going to provide much value unless you actively participate in discussions. Here's how you can make the most of your membership:

1. **Engage Authentically:** Share your thoughts, ask questions, and offer your opinions in discussions. People do business with people they trust, so be sure that comes through in your posts.
2. **Consistent Presence:** Once you choose your groups, consistently check in on them, involve yourself in active discussions, and continue to participate. Consistent involvement will help you become an integral part of the community.
3. **Avoid Over-Promotion:** Remember, while you're there to show what you know, you don't want to come off as a salesman. Stick to adding value to discussions, campaigns, or calls to action.
4. **Connect Personally:** If somebody makes a great comment or seems like they might make a great business partner or collaborator based on their insight, don't be afraid to connect with them personally, either in the group or via email. You'd be amazed at the LinkedIn business discussions that take place via group discussions and comments.
5. **Respect Group Rules:** Each group has different rules. Take the time to understand and follow them to ensure you build a respectful and professional reputation with the group.

LinkedIn Groups offer a unique way for small business owners to demonstrate thought leadership, remain informed, and form business development connections. By choosing the right groups and participating in them effectively, you can open your business to a world of opportunities in the digital space. So, jump into the world of LinkedIn Groups with fervor and watch your business grow in the digital landscape.

Chapter 36. Content Marketing on LinkedIn

After first optimizing your LinkedIn profile, the most important thing you can do on LinkedIn is to share helpful, interesting content. This content should center around your industry, not just your brand. To attract your ideal customers, your content must help them learn about, or solve a problem they have, within the industry your company does business in. You want your content to be specific enough to only attract your ideal customers. When you look at the LinkedIn pages of successful businesses, you will see a feed full of extremely good information that draws the companies' ideal customers to their page, and more importantly to their business.

Importance of Content Marketing

Content marketing not only draws your ideal customers to your business, but it helps to educate them and give them confidence in your company. Posting great content positions your company as an expert in your field, answers questions, and helps bring your ideal customers one step closer to being buyers. It's also much cheaper and more effective than traditional forms of advertising and can provide greater return on investment (ROI.)

Types of Content to Share

LinkedIn offers different types of content, including:

1. **Articles:** You can write long-form articles directly on LinkedIn. Why does this matter? Long-form articles showcase your expertise in your chosen field and can help

identify you as a thought leader.

2. **Posts:** These are short posts that are written to attract your ideal customers. These could be updates about your company, industry news, or helpful tips.

3. **Video:** The most popular type of content on LinkedIn is video. By sharing videos, which are 20 times more likely to be shared than other types of content, you can reach a much broader audience.

4. **Infographics and SlideShares:** Perfect for presenting statistics, data, and/or step-by-step guides.

Best Practices for Sharing Content

Here are some important things to keep in mind.

1. **Understand Your Audience:** It's important to know who your ideal customers are and what interests them. This will greatly assist you in choosing the best content for posts.

2. **Consistency:** Probably the most important thing you can do is to post consistently. This will help your audience to interact more with your posts and come back to your page more often.

3. **Quality Over Quantity:** Only share well-crafted, helpful, useful content. This helps to position your business as an expert in your field.

4. **Engage with Your Audience:** Make sure to reply to all comments and messages.

5. **Use Visuals:** Always include a nice visual with your LinkedIn post, as they get better engagement than text-only posts.

Content marketing on LinkedIn is a valuable outlet for small businesses. By understanding the importance of content marketing, types of content, and best practices for sharing, you can nail your content marketing and make LinkedIn a key player in your marketing efforts.

Chapter 37. LinkedIn Advertising

Welcome to the world's biggest professional playground: LinkedIn Ads, the secret weapon hiding in plain sight. LinkedIn is an incredible asset for targeting qualified leads, building brand awareness, and any B2B businesses.

Overview of LinkedIn's Advertising Platform

Imagine this: focusing on your dream customer. Here, you can narrow your audience down to their job title, company size, or even the skills listed on their profile. That's the power of LinkedIn Ads. Think about it. When you see an ad on Facebook or Instagram, it may feel like a random billboard on a freeway (if it was not properly targeted to an audience.) When your ad is properly targeted on LinkedIn, it's displayed to people who are specifically interested in what you have to offer.

This is how it works. You create your ad — choose an eye-catching image, write an irresistible headline, and add a link to your website — select your target audience, set your budget, and let LinkedIn's algorithm work its magic. Your ad will be displayed across the platform; in sponsored content pieces in newsfeeds, text ads on the sidebar, or even dynamic ads tailored to your viewers.

Different Types of LinkedIn Ads

You have several types of ads to choose from. Look through the information below to learn which type might work best for your particular goals:

- **Sponsored Content:** These are regular LinkedIn posts, given superpowers. They can be an image, video, or you can even create a carousel to showcase your product or service. These seamlessly blend into newsfeeds, so you'll capture attention without coming off as intrusive.

- **Text Ads:** Think of these as mini billboards in the LinkedIn sidebar. These are just for quick clicks to your website or a landing page you've been itching for the world to see. Lastly, LinkedIn has some great features that aren't found on other social media platforms. Take advantage of them to supercharge the return on your advertising investment!
- **Dynamic Ads:** This type of ad is automatically customized to the individual viewer. Imagine your picture alongside a headline, "Hey [Name], I see you're interested in [relevant topic]. Check out my awesome solution." (Like a virtual handshake with a personalized touch!)
- **Sponsored Messaging:** Ever received a direct message from a business on LinkedIn? It's sponsored messaging! A terrific way to reach potential customers to offer something highly relevant or start a conversation.

Tips for Effective LinkedIn Advertising

All right, here are the golden nuggets of your LinkedIn Ad campaign. Make them stand out and be prize worthy:

- **Know Your Audience:** What type of people are you trying to reach? What is their job title? What are their pain points? The more specific the better.
- **Craft Compelling Visuals And Copy:** Your ad is like an elevator pitch. Grab their attention with strong visuals and an irresistible headline. Then, in the ad copy, explain how you solve their problems and why they should care.
- **Track And Analyze:** Make sure to keep an eye on your ads'

results. Check on your ad performance and see what's working, and what's not, and adjust your targeting and budget accordingly. Remember, data is your friend. Use this amazing information to help guide your ad campaigns going forward.

- **Experiment And Have Fun!** Try different ad formats, test headlines, and maybe even a video. See which type and style of content is most popular with your audience. Continue to make small tweaks until you find what works best.

There you have it – LinkedIn Ads has your small business on the right track to advertising success. Armed with the knowledge of your audience, compelling messaging, and insight into analyzing your results, you're ready to make this professional platform work for your small business. With that, you're ready to embark on your journey to advertising greatness and show the world just how amazing your small business is!

Don't forget – there's an enormous expanse in the world of LinkedIn Ads, so keep exploring, keep concentrating, and keep pushing the boundaries. And foremost, have fun! When you're passionate about your business, it's infectious– and that's the magic that turns clicks into customers.

Chapter 38. Measuring Success

In the dynamic world of digital marketing, it's not enough to just have a LinkedIn presence. You need to understand how your activities on LinkedIn may contribute to your small business' success. This chapter will help small business owners understand how success is measured on LinkedIn. It will also provide tools to help analyze the effectiveness of their efforts and optimize their LinkedIn strategies for the best results.

Overview of LinkedIn Analytics

LinkedIn Analytics is your north star in the professional networking galaxy. It allows you to see how your content and engagement are doing, in turn, allowing you to make data-driven decisions for your small business. LinkedIn Analytics will show you information about the people who are viewing your content, how they are finding it, and which content they like best. This is how you access LinkedIn Analytics:

1. **Go to Your LinkedIn Page**
2. **Click on the Analytics Tab**

It will show you key metrics you should be watching like page views, follower demographics, and post analytics. It is important to grasp the meaning of these insights so you can decide whether your efforts are paying off.

Key Metrics to Track

1. **Impressions and Reach:** These metrics tell you how many people saw—and how far your content has traveled.

Impressions are the total number of times your content was displayed while reach is the number of unique users on LinkedIn who saw it. Monitoring both will tell you how visible your small business is on the platform.

2. **Engagement Rate:** This is how much your content was interacted with, which includes likes, comments, shares, and clicks. A high engagement rate tells you that you've given your audience something valuable and compelling. Watch which topics of posts are popular with your audience so you can give them more of what they like.

3. **Follower Growth:** Keep an eye on how your follower numbers are growing. If they're continuously growing, things are going well, and people are resonating with your content. Also, check out your new follower demographics. This will help you better understand who your evolving audience is so that you can change your LinkedIn strategy as necessary, to keep up with their interests.

How to Use Data to Refine LinkedIn Strategy

Data is the compass; interpreting what the data is telling you is the art. Once you have these insights from LinkedIn Analytics, you can improve your strategy.

- **Identify Top-Performing Content:** Get to know which of your posts your audience liked the best. What is your audience most interested in – educational content, industry intel, a look behind the curtain at your business? Now that you know, adapt your new content to match. Knowing what type of content works best with your ideal customers will help you to create more of what works.

- **Optimize Posting Times:** LinkedIn Analytics will also tell you when your audience is most often on the platform. Be sure to post then to get maximum visibility, and, hopefully, interaction. Play around with this, too, to see if there is a time of day, and day of the week, that your posts do best.

- **Adjust Your Content Mix:** Mix up post types that have been working for you, and those that have not. Adjust your mix as necessary. You'll always want to have a mix of promotional as well as informative and engaging posts on your LinkedIn Page.

Measuring success on LinkedIn is an art. You must understand the analytics, track the right key performance indicators, and then adjust your strategy based on those insights, using your best judgment. Keep an eye on your performance consistently and change as necessary and you'll help your small business go places in the professional realm of LinkedIn. Data is power – wield it!

Chapter 39. Case Studies

Of course, the platform that small businesses are best positioned to exploit is LinkedIn. As we delve into our set of case studies, we'll look at examples of how LinkedIn can work for different types of businesses.

Small Businesses Dominating on LinkedIn

1. The Artisan Bakery – From Bread Makers to Tale Tellers:
    a. **Background:** A small artisanal bakery was one of the many struggling with how to set their business apart, in a marketplace full to the brim with competitors.
    b. **LinkedIn Strategy:** The bakery began using LinkedIn to cut through the noise and allowed their potential customers to see the smiles behind each of their products. From the bakers themselves to the locally sourced ingredients, they made sure that every story was told. And they did so very, very well.
    c. **Outcome:** These 'bread makers' become 'tale tellers' and the engagement rate from their LinkedIn posts went through the roof as a result. Foot traffic increased, long-term customers became more frequent, and online orders grew as buyers across the city and beyond discovered this delicious gem!
2. Tech Startup XYZ – Bringing Thought Leadership to the Masses:
    a. **Background:** A tech startup was looking for a way to stand out in an ocean awash with new companies seeking market recognition.
    b. **LinkedIn Strategy:** The company's CEO took to

the platform himself. He shared a constant stream of thoughtful realizations, thoughtful industry-changing trends, and thoughtful solutions to the most thought-provoking questions.

   c. **Outcome:** His company found itself as the first call for partnerships from businesses that thought the same way.

3. Eco-Friendly Fashion Boutique - Join the Movement:
   a. **Background:** This sustainable fashion boutique was ready to join forces with the sustainable fashion community.
   b. **LinkedIn Strategy:** The business focused on ways of becoming ingrained into the community of eco-conscious shoppers. They shared daily environmentally friendly 'quick tips' with their followers. They explained the process of design, manufacturing, and delivery through a series of video tours of the factory. They gave voice to their customers who sought to share their stories about why they had decided to join the movement.
   c. **Outcome:** Their followers not only bought and bought more often than any of their other customers, but they also led sustainability discussions on the boutique's LinkedIn Page.

Lessons Learned from these Case Studies

So, here are a few key lessons you can take away from these success stories:

1. **Authenticity Matters:** These case studies illustrate that authenticity pays off. For small businesses, LinkedIn is a channel for sharing your unique story and the values behind

your business. Let the more human side of your brand shine through, and you'll build the kind of trust that lasts.

2. **Consistency is Key:** The successful outcomes for all these brands demonstrate the importance of maintaining a steady schedule of LinkedIn engagement. Whether you're sharing updates, insight from your industry, or a sneak peek behind the scenes, regularly providing reasons for your audience to come back, keeps them engaged and invested in your small business.

3. **Build a Community:** Of course, it's more than just posting content. Take the time to respond to the comments you do get and take advantage of the ability to ask for your followers' opinions. Building a community around your small business on LinkedIn (and any social network) is the ultimate way to make your followers feel a part of something bigger.

4. **Position Yourself as an Authority:** It's so vital to being successful on the 'world's largest professional networking site' that you'll find it woven through all the case studies. Sharing insights, solutions and your expertise will not only bring customers to you, but other businesses will be knocking at your door for possible partnerships, too.

The outcomes may vary slightly depending on your industry, but there's no denying the impact LinkedIn can have on small businesses that approach the platform the right way. Just remember success isn't only measured in numbers. Like Gabrielle Mautone from FreeTime Fitness says, "It's not about followers or connections; it's about the relationship to the individuals and the community." So go ahead, let these stories inspire you, and see where LinkedIn can take your small business.

Chapter 40. Conclusion

Congratulations on reaching the final chapter of this book! You've taken a significant stride towards harnessing the full power of LinkedIn for your small business. As we close out on this chapter of our journey together, let's take a moment to revisit some of the key insights and strategies we've covered, and then get some words of inspiration to light your way on your LinkedIn marketing journey.

Recap of the Book: Exploring the LinkedIn Landscape

In the opening chapters, we delved into the essentials of creating a powerful LinkedIn profile. Remember, this is more than just a resume; it is your digital storefront. Post a magnetic headline, showcase your top skills, and ensure that your profile image echoes the ethos of your business.

We dug into the tried-and-true principles of building a top-shelf network. Bolster your connections with peers, clients, and industry game changers. Remember, the might of your LinkedIn network is about much more than the numbers; it's about the value of the relationships you build.

Content reigns supreme on LinkedIn. Deliver valuable, industry-relevant pieces that slot you directly into the expert column. Get into the discussion with your audience via posts, articles, and comments. Keep your business at the forefront by tapping in with regular updates.

And don't forget about LinkedIn Groups. These little goldmines are dynamically focused. Dive into groups specific to your industry, lend your expertise to active discussions, and don't discount how building your network within these side scenes also demonstrates your expert stripes.

We made time to pivot into the robust metrics that LinkedIn can deliver to you. Review your engagement metrics. Track your adjustments. And maintain the unflagging adaptability you'll need to keep your LinkedIn marketing ship tight as it whips through the ever-shifting social media marketing straits.

Encouragement for Small Business Owners: Your Journey Continues

For small business owners, this journey isn't concluded here—it's just the beginning. Keep pressing forward and hold fast to the simple understanding: Success on LinkedIn is a long play. Build an impactful presence and cultivate connections that pay off. Remember, all of this takes time.

This is not merely a digital resume; it's an electricity field of chances. Let go and be brave while sharing your unique brand narrative. It's reachable highs and the sometimes-bittersweet lessons learned. This type of truthfulness builds trust and trust is everything for forming enduring business relationships.

Don't be shy about popping open the lid on LinkedIn's myriad of advanced features. Play with them and learn, which jumpstarts your unique small business.

Lastly, of course, remember: This is never about you. This is about all of us, collaborating in this small fishpond. Be genuine in your connections. Toast their wins. Lend an ear when they need it. Building a network that thrives is contingent on this.

Part 5. YouTube | Chapter 41. Introduction

Marketing has changed drastically over the last decade, and one of the main reasons for this is the digital age. YouTube has been key to this change as we continue to see the platform make headlines. With over 2 billion logged-in users a month, the video-sharing platform is so much more than a place to create; it's one of the best marketing tools small businesses have to reach a global audience.

So why is YouTube so important in digital marketing? As mentioned above, the two billion users a month is a strong start, but the nature of video content is where it really shines. Yes, text and images can be great, but videos allow customers to see products or services in action. As a result, this makes it easier for potential buyers to understand what businesses are offering. Additionally, YouTube's algorithm is incredibly helpful for businesses. The system recommends different videos applicable to users based on the content they've watched, so it's easier for businesses to reach the demographic they're looking for.

An engagement aspect can also be a major factor in YouTube's role in digital marketing; the direct interaction with viewers. People can comment, like, and share videos as they want, which allows businesses to become part of a brand community. With the right strategy, this can lead to a more loyal customer base and increased word-of-mouth referrals.

Among this incredible reach are many people who watch YouTube every single day and these are people looking to learn something, entertain themselves, and discover products. They want to connect with brands and one of the best ways to do just that is through storytelling. Video content is just about the most ideal form of consumption there is for brands. It's engaging for viewers and has the potential to deliver a ton of information in a short time. Most of all, it helps your customer to understand you as a brand, which can be pretty challenging with the written word.

Chapter 42. Understanding YouTube

YouTube is a website and app that allows you to share videos for free. YouTube is owned by Google, which is the largest search engine in the world. The platform has two types of users: video creators who create a YouTube channel and upload videos to it – and viewers who create an account on the platform for the purpose of watching and interacting with videos. YouTube is for everyone — from the individual looking for entertainment or answers to their questions, to the head of a major corporation with a large budget to run ads on the platform. You can access YouTube in more than 80 languages and from almost every country in the world. Wondering as a small business owner why you should even be interested in marketing on YouTube? Take a look at these YouTube statistics:

YouTube Statistics

- YouTube has 2.5 billion users worldwide.
- 82% of US adults use YouTube. (source: Hootsuite)
- YouTube is the second most popular search engine after Google.
- YouTube is available in 100 countries and 80 different languages.
- People watch more than 1 billion hours of video on the platform, every day.
- 62% of businesses use YouTube.
- 63% of consumers have watched YouTube on a mobile device.
- 26% of consumers say they discover products through YouTube ads.
- 500 hours of video are uploaded to YouTube every minute,

worldwide.

Brief History and Evolution of YouTube

Three former PayPal employees banded together in 2005 to create a platform that would forever change the way we share and view video content. Chad Hurley, Steve Chen, and Jawed Karim founded YouTube in 2005 with a simple goal: to make it easy for people to share and discover videos. They had no idea that they were, in fact, laying the groundwork for an online communication revolution.

Since its founding in 2005, YouTube has gone from being a platform for sharing home videos to being the stage of choice for creators, businesses, and influencers. Google saw its potential and bought it in 2006, taking it to new heights. Today, over 2 billion logged-in, monthly users come to YouTube to enjoy the video content they love, making it the second-largest search engine worldwide. It's not just a platform; it's a community, an entertainment hub, a source for finding answers to questions and it has become an essential tool for marketing for businesses of all sizes.

Why YouTube Is Important for Businesses

So, why should small business owners like yourself care about YouTube? It's simple: attention. In a world where everyone and everything is vying for the attention of internet users, YouTube offers an incredible opportunity to attract it through thoughtful and engaging video content. We've reached a point where watching videos is the preferred method of consuming information, and YouTube is the destination of choice for the over 2 billion users who come every month to learn, be entertained, and have their problems solved.

The platform provides businesses with the ability to show off their products, tell their brand story, and reach a worldwide audience. With

YouTube Ads, you can choose the precise audience where your message will be most relevant, making sure that it gets in front of the right people, at the right time. You can use the platform to create tutorials, give glimpses from behind the scenes, or create light-hearted content that your audience will love to eat up.

An Overview of YouTube's User Base and Demographics

Knowing your audience is key to having true success with any and all marketing, and YouTube's user base is as diverse as it gets. From tweens looking for the next viral trend to professionals who are looking to learn everything they can about marketing, accounting, or computer programming, there's a corner of the net for everyone.

Over 50% of YouTube users are now aged 35 and up. If you're looking to connect with millennials, Gen Xers, or Baby Boomers, YouTube is where you want to connect with them authentically. With content available in over 80 languages, YouTube is a truly global platform to help expand your business across the world.

It's a dynamic ecosystem where small businesses can find huge opportunities. As you step into the world of YouTube, however, understand it's a platform that has evolved, understand the power it holds, and embrace the sheer diversity of its user base. The world of YouTube is huge and with the right approach, so too are the possibilities for your small business in this digital landscape.

Chapter 43. Setting Up Your YouTube Channel

YouTube can be an incredible source of traffic, leads, and sales. It's a way to introduce your small business to the world. You can tell the world about your business, present your products or services, and connect with your customer base. In short, it's a must. Here's how to build a YouTube channel for your small business:

- **Create a Google Account:** If you don't have one already, you'll need a Google account. This is required to be able to create a YouTube channel. If you created a Gmail account, signed up for Google+ in the past, or used any other Google service, you already have an account.
- **Create a YouTube Channel:** Now that you have a Google account, go to YouTube and sign in. Click on your profile picture, then in the top right corner, click on "Create a channel. "Follow the prompts to create a name for your channel and add a description. Click "Done" when you're finished and you're ready to go.

A Step-by-Step Guide to Creating a YouTube Channel for Your Small Business

- **Sign in to YouTube:** Use your Google account to sign in to YouTube.
- **Go to Your Channel List:** Click on your profile icon in the top-right corner and click on "Your channel."
- **Create a New Channel:** Click "Create a new channel," then choose a name for your new channel.

- **Customize Your Channel:** Add a channel description here. You can also add links to your business website and social media channels, here.

A Few Tips for Choosing a Channel Name and Description

Your channel name and description are two of the most important things on your YouTube presence. They tell users who you are and what you're about, and they help you show up in user searches.

- **Channel Name:** Your channel name should be closely associated with your small business, easy to remember, and easy to spell. In many cases, this should be your business name.
- **Description:** Your channel description will tell visitors what your business is all about and what people can expect from your videos. It should be clear and tell users everything they need to know to understand your channel. Be sure to add the keywords that your ideal customers are most likely to use when searching for a business like yours.

Having the Right Channel Art and How to Create It

What do we mean by channel art? Your profile picture and banner image. This is the first thing that viewers will see when they come to your channel for the first time. It's your chance to leave a strong first impression.

- **Profile Picture:** This should be your business's logo. The recommended picture size is 800 x 800 pixels.
- **Banner Image:** This is a bigger picture at the top of your YouTube channel. Use this to say more about your business. You might want to use it to tell what your business does,

promote an event, or run a promotion. The recommended image size is 2560 x 1440 pixels.

- **First Impressions Matter:** The first thing that visitors will notice is your channel art. Your channel's profile picture and banner are the showcases for your brand. So, use high-quality images that match your small business's aesthetic.

- **Channel Icon:** Your profile picture will appear even when you leave comments. This should always be your company's logo. It's important to keep this logo as the profile picture across all social media platforms so that your followers can be sure they have found you, online.

- **Free design tools:** Don't have any designer's skills at all? No problem. There are free tools like Canva or Adobe Spark that have a bunch of templates. They are very easy to use, even for beginners.

Just remember to keep your branding consistent and professional.

Chapter 44. Content Creation

Let's start with the first critical element of YouTube marketing: creating engaging content. Content is truly king for YouTube marketing success. It's not just about the innumerable videos you may be tempted to create, but rather focusing on the quality. High-quality content is more likely to attract viewers, encourage sharing, and promote viewer interaction. And these are all things critical to your heightened presence on YouTube.

Understanding What Content Works on YouTube

YouTube is a melting pot where education and entertainment come together. You'll notice this, as most successful content on YouTube either teaches something or enriches the viewer in some way. Sometimes that education is as simple as providing the viewer with an enjoyable experience. When attempting to understand what content works here, take the time to review popular videos in your industry: What is the format? What are the trends and themes? How can you apply these insights to your content? Whether it's tutorials, peeks behind the scenes, or storytelling about your business journey, make sure to align your content with what your audience wants.

How-To Plan and Script Videos

Having a plan and a script for your YouTube videos makes sure your message is clear and concise. Once you've established your video's purpose, your target audience, and what you want them to do, you can decide how to script it. The big thing is that you can't just wing it. Start with an outline and you can keep from fumbling your way through the video. Outlines can help keep it short; keep it tight and keep you from rambling. Even if you are reading from a script, which I don't recommend, you should never look or sound like you're reading. Be yourself, and it's much more likely to come off as authentic. In addition, authenticity is extremely important when it comes to YouTube marketing.

Basics of Filming and Editing Videos

You don't need a professional studio to film a YouTube video. A quiet, well-lit place and a decent smartphone (with earbuds) or video camera with a decent microphone, are enough to get started. Pay attention to lighting and sound quality. Good lighting enhances the viewer experience; however, you don't need to buy studio lights. The biggest part of lighting is the magic hour, which happens twice a day, once in the morning and once in the afternoon. The light during the magic hours is both soft and warm, and either enhances or eliminates harsh shadows entirely. Where sound is concerned, a basic digital video camera will have a microphone that's good enough for filming.

When it comes to editing, you'll make fast and easy work of the process thanks to several user-friendly editing tools that are available. Even beginners can get the hang of editing, with a little practice. Just remember as mentioned earlier, done is much better than perfect. Most people would rather watch an authentic person sharing content than something that's highly polished. Keep your videos both pretty short and overwhelmingly engaging, as viewer retention is necessary for YouTube's algorithm.

The Importance of Thumbnails and How to Design Them

The thumbnail is the first thing potential viewers will see. A captivating thumbnail can do wonders for your video's CTR (click-through rate). There are various tutorials throughout both YouTube and Google that'll show you how to create your customized thumbnails. Consider a program like Canva for creating your thumbnails. Canva has many templates available, and most of Canva's features are free to use.

Thumbnails should be really vibrant and always inviting. This can be accomplished by numerous things like using bold text, and warm bright hues. Make sure your background is not too dark colored or busy so that your text shows clearly. Play around with various hues to figure out which effect you like best. After your thumbnail has been uploaded to YouTube's main system, this is generally what will happen next.

Chapter 45. Optimizing Your Videos

Optimizing your videos is the key to success on this platform. Optimization simply refers to making your content more discoverable and more appealing to your current audience and potential customers. Let's start with the basics. Focus on video quality, lighting, and sound. A clear, well-lit video with great audio is more likely to engage viewers. Remember, first impressions are important, so take the time to create visually appealing content.

YouTube SEO

YouTube SEO (Search Engine Optimization) is about making your videos discoverable by users who are searching for content like yours. This includes optimizing your channel, playlists, metadata (data that helps to sort and identify your videos,) description, and a few more techy-sounding concepts. Understanding the YouTube search algorithm is the only way your videos will ever get seen. The algorithm searches for many factors to determine your video rank. These include keywords used in titles, descriptions, tags, engagement, and video quality. Start by identifying a few keywords that are related to your business and include these key terms in your video titles, descriptions, and tags. This helps paint a more vivid picture of what your content is about and increases the likelihood of your videos showing up in search results. Crafting an effective title, description, and tag can give your videos the exposure they need to accelerate your YouTube marketing and increase your business.

How to Write Effective Titles, Descriptions, and Tags

The title, description, and tags can make or break your video in the search results. Proper titles are very important when it comes to getting your video clicked on. A title should be concise, descriptive, and include the most important keywords. As with all the previously mentioned digital trends, titles are the first thing a user sees when they are browsing, so make them count.

Your description allows you to give searchers more context about your video. Searchers need to know what it is about so they can tell whether or not it applies to them. You will want to include some important information about the video, as well as give your video some personality. Don't be too informational, be engaging and have fun. Do include the main keywords in the description in a natural way, this can help your videos rank higher and increase your views.

Captions and Subtitles

Closed captions and subtitles aren't just for those who are hearing impaired. They can make your content more accessible. They go hand and hand with YouTube SEO. A closed caption lets you include the YouTube-generated video transcript that's been synced to your video. This will more than likely spike up your YouTube SEO, which we will get to in a little bit. We know what you're thinking, all videos are automatically transcribed, aren't they? They're not. If YouTube can't hear what you're saying, they'll record "(inaudible 23:45)," and rank your video lower than those with actual transcripts. As always, YouTube wants us to give'em more.

Why captions and transcripts increase YouTube's SEO

Your video is more likely to show up in results if you have keywords in your closed captions.

Don't stop there. A LOT of people turn on videos with closed captions and watch them at work, out of consideration for their co-workers and their own privacy.

These words will help if YouTube can't hear/understand/make out any words in your video.

Strictly for the hearing impaired

They show that the content creator made a gallant effort to go above and beyond for their following. It turns your video content into something more amazing. By providing that for your audience, you enhance their experience, and we both know you wouldn't have it any other way.

Chapter 46. Growing Your Channel

Now that we've talked about how to create a YouTube channel, let's discuss how to grow your audience. Nothing happens overnight and your YouTube channel will take time to grow. Remember: patience and persistence are key. The first thing you need to do is to understand who your ideal customers are. Think about what they need. What problems do they want to solve? Make sure the entire video is filled with valuable content.

One of the best ways to connect your views and bring them one step closer to being buyers is by answering all messages and replying to all comments. Building a community on your channel will help a lot.

How Calls to Action Work

YouTube "calls to action" (CTA's) are one of your best friends for subscriber growth. Let your viewers know how to like, subscribe, and share your videos. You can also use calls to action to ask your viewers to enter a contest, watch another video, or check out your sale.

The perfect place for your CTA might be at the end of the video. If your videos are in the middle of a series you're doing (or suspenseful enough for this type of video series), then you can ask viewers to look at your playlists so they can watch the other videos in the series. Wanting to get comments on your video? Ask your viewers a question in the video, then tell them to leave their reply in the comments.

Make sure to end your videos with a compelling CTA. Whether it's asking your viewers a question, prompting a discussion in the comments, or asking them to check out your latest offerings, make sure you're keeping them engaged beyond simply watching the video.

Concluding Remarks for Business Owners on YouTube

Consistency and a regular posting schedule are crucial. Plan your content in advance and get your videos scheduled. This way there's a variety of topics and you won't be posting content that gets old quickly. For example, it might not make sense for a small business to be posting about a sale they put on in February, come November – even if it's the best sale you've ever run. Post regularly to keep your audience engaged and this will also show YouTube's algorithms that your channel is active and can be counted on to provide consistent content. Doing so can improve the video's visibility in search results and recommended videos.

Creating a successful business on YouTube is not incredibly dissimilar to creating a successful business in general. It comes down to a few core principles: create valuable content, be consistent, promote your videos, and market in a consistent and high-quality way. Work hard to create videos that are interesting, informative, and helpful, and don't necessarily be so sales and brand-loyalty-focused that you wind up coming across as extra salesy. According to Google, ninety percent of viewers think that authenticity is the most important factor when they're deciding whether they'll keep viewing content. Also, encourage viewers to subscribe to make sure they don't miss anything that's coming. Also ask them to hit the Like button, share, and comment on your videos. Getting more comments doesn't just make the video look more popular and increase its apparent quality, it can also improve the video's ranking on YouTube.

Tips for Promoting Your Channel and Videos

Not happy with the number of views your videos are getting? Here are some things you can do to get more views. Promote your videos through other channels. Share them on your social profiles, in newsletters to your email subscribers, and of course, on your website.

Reach out to have your videos featured by other outlets, and if you have good relationships with other small businesses or with influencers in your niche, ask if there are opportunities for them to promote your videos in exchange for a shout-out from you.

Work to optimize your videos for discovery. YouTube is incredibly form and topic-sensitive. Make sure to include the most common terms that your ideal customers use when looking for your products or services. Adding these terms (or keywords) to your tiles, descriptions, and tags can help your videos show up higher in search rankings and recommended video lists.

You should also ask your viewers to share your videos. Word of mouth can be a powerful marketing tool and positive recommendations from people in your audience can be a big part of how a channel grows.

Remember, growing a YouTube channel takes time and consistency. Stay true to your brand, consistently deliver quality content, and actively promote your videos to help your small business grow in the digital world.

Chapter 47. Engaging with Your Audience

Engaging with Your Audience

In the vast world of YouTube, engaging with your audience is not just a good practice – it's a game-changer for your small business. Imagine YouTube as a bustling marketplace, and your engagement as the friendly business owner eager to chat with customers. Doing so will help you to build loyalty and trust in your small business.

When you create content, remember that your audience isn't just a faceless viewer. They're real people with thoughts, opinions, and a desire to connect. Respond to comments, ask for feedback, and ask viewers to like and comment on your videos. This sense of fellowship keeps viewers engaged and keeps them coming back to your small business. When you involve your audience, they become invested in your brand.

Importance of Engagement in YouTube's Algorithm

The YouTube algorithm is a beast of untold complexity, but one thing is for sure – it loves engagement. When viewers like, comment, and subscribe, it notifies the YouTube algorithm that your content is good, and that people are interested in it. The more your viewers interact with your videos, the more YouTube shares them with new viewers.

Ask your audience to like and comment on your videos. The comments section is an excellent place for viewers to congregate and chat about your content. This interaction is an endorsement in the eyes of the algorithm. Valuable interaction boosts your video's visibility, and your small business, to new heights.

How to Manage and Respond to Comments

Managing and responding to comments can seem daunting, especially when you're receiving a high volume. The comments section is the digital storefront of your video, where customers express their thoughts. Compliments, questions, or even constructive criticism – these words are important. They show that you are attentive, working to improve, and participating in the conversation.

Set aside some time regularly to read over comments. Respond to questions, say thank you for positive comments, and address concerns kindly. The purpose is not just to have comments, but to have a thriving community around your brand.

Using YouTube's Community Features

YouTube offers several community features for this very purpose. Under the community tab, you can post events, polls, or just fun glimpses from behind the scenes. Polls are an excellent way for users to interact with your brand, and to ask them what they like. Whether it's choosing your favorite product, or maybe even the topic of your next video, polls help viewers feel like they're part of the team.

Investigate the YouTube channel membership program, where you offer memberships to your most dedicated subscribers. Early access to videos, special badges, and members-only live chats are just a few of the perks that you can offer. These features make your viewers feel special and have the added bonus of boosting your revenue. Remember – the more you reach out, the more your audience will respond. As you grow a loyal community around your brand, your visibility on YouTube will increase. This is how you successfully market your small business.

Chapter 48. Monetizing Your Channel

Monetizing your YouTube channel involves turning your channel into a revenue stream by enabling ads on your videos and earning money from ad revenue. Here are the best practices to follow. Before you start dreaming of four-figure paychecks, you'll need to get your channel approved for monetization. And that means following the rules.

An Overview of YouTube's Partner Program

The YouTube Partner Program (YPP) allows creators to share the money earned from ads displayed on their videos. To join the YPP, your channel needs to have 1,000 subscribers and 4,000 hours of watch time in the past 12 months, then you can apply. If accepted, you can start making money from the ads on your videos. YouTube pays a portion of the ad revenue to the channel, and the channel also makes money from YouTube Premium subscribers watching their content.

Remember, growing your YouTube channel takes time! Building to 1,000 subscribers and 4,000 hours of watch time takes patience but try to enjoy the journey and make quality content that your target audience will find valuable.

Other Monetization Strategies

In addition to the YouTube Partner Program, other common monetization strategies to consider are:

- **Merchandise:** Use your branding to sell merchandise related to your business, such as t-shirts, mugs, or anything your audience would love. Platforms like Teespring integrate with YouTube to make showcasing and selling your merchandise easy.

- **Patreon:** Patreon is a platform that lets your fans support you directly. You can provide exclusive content for patrons only, behind-the-scenes access, and other perks in exchange for a small monthly subscription fee. It's a great way to build a community around your brand.
- **Sponsored Videos:** Making sponsored videos for brands can be very lucrative, as they may pay you to feature their products or services. Make sure it aligns with your values and benefits your viewers. It's crucial to disclose in your video if it is sponsored.

Chapter 49. Analyzing Your Performance

YouTube Analytics is like a VIP pass to the inner workings of your channel: It serves up a wealth of insights on your audience, their behavior, and the impact of your content. Here's how to find it: Click on your profile picture at the top right, then select "YouTube Studio." When you arrive at your screen, just click the "Analytics" tab.

Once you click on it, you'll see a lot of numbers, like watch time, your views, how many subscribers you've gained, and more. So, let's break down a few key metrics, and look at what they mean for your company.

Key Metrics to Track and How to Interpret Them

- **Watch Time:** This figure tallies the total number of minutes viewers have watched your videos. A higher watch time is a sign your content is engaging, and viewers are sticking around.
- **Views:** This is a simple one — it's just the number of times your videos have been watched. While seeing high view counts is exciting, pay close attention to watch time first, as it's a greater reflection of quality and relevance.
- **Subscribers:** This is simply the count of everyone who has subscribed to your channel. Keeping an eye on this count is the best indication of how your channel is growing: If that number is going up, your content resonates with your audience.
- **Click-Through Rate (CTR):** Your CTR is the percentage of people who clicked on your video after they saw your thumbnail. A higher CTR means your video is doing a good job getting people to click since either your thumbnail, title

or both are compelling to viewers.

- **Audience Retention:** This metric shows the average percentage of a video that viewers watch. The higher this percentage, the more of your video people are watching. It's great to get a feel for this metric for individual videos, but looking at the average audience retention of your videos can give you a rough estimate of quality over time. This helps you to see where your videos can be improved.

How to Use Data to Improve Your Content and Strategy

With these now-common metrics in hand, it's time to put them to work for your channel. Here are some quick hit ways to use YouTube Analytics data to improve your content and strategy:

- **Identify Top-Performing Content:** Look at the videos with your highest watch time, views, and, most importantly, engagement. Are there common themes here? What can you replicate in your upcoming videos?
- **Understand Your Audience:** Flip over to the "Audience" tab to get a read on the general demographics and interests of your audience. Then, customize your content to them so it stays relevant and engaging.
- **Optimize Thumbnails and Titles:** Check out videos with high CTRs in the "Click-Through Rate" tab, in the "Overview" drop-down. What is it about these videos' thumbnails and titles that make them successful? Try working on different designs and learn the ones that maximize views and engagement.
- **Address Drop-off Points:** As you watch your video, check to see where audience retention plummets. Are those points in your video too long? Are certain sections less interesting? Edit them down to keep your viewers captivated throughout.

Just remember: YouTube analytics is an ongoing conversation, not a one-time thing. Keep checking your metrics to monitor your performance, adapt your strategy to maintain and increase your success and, with a bit of data-driven magic, you'll be dominating YouTube like a pro in no time!

Chapter 50. Case Studies

Case Studies: How Small Businesses Can Kill It on YouTube

In this section, we look at some examples of how small businesses can use YouTube to increase their bottom line and take their business to the next level. These case studies show how different entrepreneurs can leverage the platform to their advantage. You'll see that YouTube isn't just for the big players, it's just as powerful of a tool for small businesses!

Case Study 1: The Artisan Bakery

Meet Emily, a small, local artisan baker who has opened a shop in a small, cozy corner of town. She realized that everyone loves to watch her craft and more specifically her mouth-watering baked goods. She started a YouTube channel to show consumers just how much went into making her beautiful and sweet confections. Through engaging videos, she would not only show baking demonstrations but would tell inviting stories about each of her confections. She also talked about herself, which was hugely endearing to her loyal following.

Result: Emily's YouTube channel became the talk of the town and beyond for foodies. She saw a bump in her online orders and in foot traffic into her bakery. This helped her establish herself as a favorite in her local community.

Key Takeaway: If you have a small business, or work with a company with a community-based clientele, being authentic and real can be incredibly valuable in gaining and keeping clients.

Case Study 2: The Tech Repair Shop

One day Jason, the owner of a small, local tech repair shop, decided he wanted to start a YouTube channel and needed some help. The tech repair space, and retail in general, is extremely competitive. Not to mention the fact that there are a ton of people recording tech repair videos from their basement, who you would have to compete with. This left Jason's shop with a few problems and left him scratching his head.

Jason decided to start with several do-it-yourself tech tips and how to troubleshoot the plethora of bugs and issues that plague techies. He also started doing reviews of the latest gadgets and tech to hit the market. Not only did this make Jason an authority in tech, but it also brought in a new type of clientele to his shop - the people that he now had watching his channel who weren't "Do It Yourselfers". These new customers ended up leaving with some sort of professional service because they believed he knew what he was talking about.

Result: Not only did this establish Jason's shop as an authority for professional services, but it also started bringing in a new clientele of people who felt they were "Do It Yourselfers". The channel became a hub for tech discussion in the community. With a team in his shop and his dedicated video editor behind the scenes, he was able to add another source of revenue to his business. Jason began to sell advertisements and videos to other companies who wanted to market their products on his channel.

Key Takeaway: Whatever industry you're in, if you're looking to sell professional services, being seen as an expert in your business can be a huge opportunity to increase your bottom line.

Case Study 3: The Fitness Studio

Next, we have the very talented Sarah, who owns a local fitness studio. She was looking to increase her clientele beyond the around-the-block radius of 5 miles or so. She taped into the entire at-home workout community that was rapidly growing. She began posting short but super-effective workout routines. The next thing she knew she was being seen as the expert at teaching people how to get in shape. The next thing she knew, she had thousands of online followers, and her success had come full circle. Sarah was now the owner of a popular brick-and-mortar fitness studio. She rolled out a line of supplements and nutritional products. She was now a brand and not just a brick-and-mortar fitness studio.

Result: Sarah now owned a fitness studio and a popular line of supplements, and she had clients from all over the world watching her videos. She had created a brand with several sources of income, that no longer relied on finding clients within a 5-mile radius of her brick-and-mortar location.

Key Takeaway: Identify trends and cater to a wider audience by offering valuable content beyond your core products or services.

As you can see there are several ways this can play out, but the point is there are so many different and unique ways to leverage YouTube. It is an incredibly powerful tool that allows large brands and small business owners alike to uniquely sell their products and services. YouTube allows you to reach a very wide audience and do so in an intimate and authentic way.

Chapter 51. Conclusion

In summary, YouTube is a valuable tool for small businesses. It provides a platform to connect with a global audience, engage with customers, and keep them informed dynamically. In short, through an understanding and application of YouTube's marketing power, small business can greatly enhance their market presence and generate a significant uptick in growth.

Keep in mind that YouTube marketing isn't just about making and uploading videos. It's about a complete strategy that aligns with your business goals. That includes an in-depth understanding of your target audience, creating compelling content, optimizing your videos for search, and engaging with your viewers.

Remember, the key is consistency. The regular creation of high-quality videos will help build an engaged subscriber base. If your users leave comments or feedback, reply to them, and address their input in future content.

Also, don't underestimate the power of a team effort. Teaming up (whether it be with influencers in your niche or other non-competing local businesses) will help you reach a wider audience. Additionally, think about trying your hand with advertisements as another way to increase visibility on YouTube.

To be clear — success on YouTube doesn't happen overnight. Be patient, be willing to put in the work and learn and adapt. Follow your performance through YouTube Analytics and use that to tweak your strategy.

Finally, it should go without saying — always remember that YouTube is a community. So don't just come howling at them trying to sell your stuff off the bat. Go there to connect, engage, and build your brand. By communicating with your viewers, you aren't just selling your small business products and services, you're building a loyal community that helps your small business to grow.

YouTube provides a great opportunity for small businesses to market themselves effectively with a limited budget. So, rejoice, embrace the video age, and let YouTube take your small business to the next level. It's a community that just may make your small business the next big thing on YouTube. And don't forget – every big business was once a small business.

Conclusion

Congratulations on reaching the conclusion of our journey through the dynamic landscape of social media marketing for small businesses. In this final chapter, let us recap the best platforms discussed throughout this book and offer insights into the evolving future of social media.

Recap of the Best Social Media Platforms

- **Facebook Marketing Strategies:** Create a compelling business page, engage with Facebook groups, and utilize advertising options to maximize your impact on this giant social media platform.

- **Instagram Marketing Tactics:** Optimize your Instagram profile, leverage visual storytelling, and explore advertising options to showcase your products or services creatively.

- **LinkedIn for B2B Marketing:** Establish a professional LinkedIn profile, engage in relevant groups, and explore sponsored content and advertising options for effective B2B marketing.

- **YouTube Marketing Strategies:** Create and optimize your YouTube channel, develop engaging video content, and explore YouTube advertising and analytics for a dynamic visual presence.

- **TikTok for the Modern Audience:** Understand the younger demographic, create engaging short-form content, and leverage advertising options on TikTok.

- **Pinterest and E-commerce:** Showcase products creatively, create visually appealing pins, and utilize Pinterest advertising to reach a visually oriented audience, particularly in e-commerce.

- **Twitter for Small Business Promotion:** Craft concise and engaging tweets, leverage hashtags strategically, and build a community through active interaction.

Insights into the Future

As we look ahead, the future of social media for small businesses is marked by continual evolution. Take advantage of new trends, such as:

- **Video Dominance:** Video will continue to be king. Short-form video and live stream video will continue to grow in popularity.
- **Ephemeral Content:** Storytelling and story form content will continue to grow in popularity.
- **Augmented Reality (AR) Experiences:** AR features in social media will offer interactive and immersive experiences, enhancing user engagement.
- **Voice Search Optimization:** With the rise of voice-activated devices, optimizing content for voice search will become crucial for online visibility.
- **Community Building:** Building authentic communities around your brand will be key. Engage with your audience, encourage user-generated content, and foster a sense of belonging.
- **Remember:** The social media landscape is dynamic, and staying adaptable to new trends and technologies will ensure your small business remains at the forefront of online marketing.

Which Social Media Platforms Are Right For You?

In this book, we demonstrated the need for all businesses, regardless of size, to have a presence on social media. We provided an overview of what we consider the seven best social media platforms, highlighting the best four, for small businesses to use to expand the marketing of their unique business. We described in detail how to get started, how to create content, and how to optimize, promote, and measure the success of each social media platform. But, by all means, establish your business presence on social media! The content of this book is also available as five eBooks on Amazon Kindle, Apple Books, Google Play and in other locations. As new titles become available, you can find them on Fox Social Media website at - https://foxsocialmedia.com/ebooks

Feeling Overwhelmed with Social Media Marketing? You are Not Alone!

We understand that diving into the world of social media marketing can be both exciting and challenging for small business owners. If you feel you need assistance with your social media marketing, fear not! Fox Social Media and its educational arm, Simple Marketing Academy, are here to simplify your journey.

Simple Marketing Academy provides podcasts and videos, for FREE, for small business owners and entrepreneurs, to help them simplify the process of marketing and growing their businesses, reaching their ideal customers, and increasing their sales. We provide comprehensive guidance on how to utilize social media, email, online advertising, and more.

Fox Social Media offers online marketing packages tailored to suit businesses of all sizes, and our dedicated team is ready to provide the support you need. From creating engaging content to managing your social media presence, we have got you covered. We can handle the intricacies while you focus on what you do best – running your business. Take the stress out of social media marketing and let Fox Social Media help you achieve success online. Visit our website or contact us today to explore how we can enhance your digital presence and drive your business forward.

Simple Marketing Academy Podcast:

https://thesmallbusinesssocialpodast.libsyn.com

Simple Marketing Academy Show on YouTube:

https://www.youtube.com/@SimpleMarketingAcademy

Website: https://foxsocialmedia.com

Email: info@foxsocialmedia.com

eBooks & Audiobooks by Jill W. Fox

Social Media Marketing Series

The Best Social Media Platforms for Small Business Marketing

Facebook Marketing Mastery: A Guide for Small Business Marketing

Unlocking Instagram: The Small Business Key to Success

LinkedIn Unleashed: Empowering Small Business Key to Success

The YouTube Advantage: Boost Your Small Business with Video

These eBooks and Audiobooks can be found at:

https://foxsocialmedia.com/ebooks

eBooks Coming Soon

eBook Idea to Worldwide Success: How to Write, Publish, and Distribute Your eBook Worldwide with Minimal Cost

eBook Promotion Mastery: The Books2Read Playbook – Exciting Promotional Tools and Beyond

eBook From Ordinary to Extraordinary: A Guide For An eBook That Stands Out

About The Author

Jill is the co-owner of Fox Social Media and an experienced Marketing Consultant for small businesses in a multitude of industries. Since 2010, Jill's been helping clients to reach their ideal customers, grow their businesses, and increase their revenue. She has set up, run, and managed the social media and advertising operations for clients in the fields of medicine, law, accounting, human resources, investment banking, education, commercial and residential real estate, sports, non-profit, restaurant, fitness, TV & film production, talent management, online retail, magazine publication, solar energy, as well as for bloggers and very high-profile individuals. Another of her passions is teaching, and she's been invited to guest lecture at prominent universities, and speak to businesses on the topic of online marketing. Jill is also the co-host of the "Simple Marketing Academy Show" on YouTube and, the "Simple Marketing Academy Podcast."

Book cover designed by MaugeDesign.online.

About The Publisher

Simple Marketing Academy, the educational arm of Fox Social Media, provides training for small business owners and entrepreneurs, to help them simplify the process of marketing and growing their businesses, reaching their ideal customers, and increasing their sales. We provide comprehensive guidance on how to utilize social media, email, online advertising, and more. Our step-by-step instructions are designed to help you master these skills swiftly. We understand that time is a precious commodity, so we'll guide you on what to focus on, enabling you to tune out the rest of the noise. Whether you're a visual learner who prefers watching (Simple Marketing Academy videos) or an auditory learner who prefers listening (Simple Marketing Academy podcasts,) we've got you covered!

We're excited to announce the launch of our first series of eBooks on Social Media Marketing for Small Businesses. As new titles become available, you can find them at https://foxsocialmedia.com/ebooks.

We look forward to supporting you on your journey to business success.